THE ANCIENT WORLD

BENIN

AND OTHER AFRICAN KINGDOMS

Sean Sheehan

WAYLAND

THE ANCIENT WORLD

THE AZTECS • BENIN AND OTHER AFRICAN KINGDOMS
EGYPT • GREECE • THE INCAS • ROME

Produced for Wayland Publishers Limited by
Roger Coote Publishing
Gissing's Farm, Fressingfield, Eye
Suffolk IP21 5SH, England

Editor: Alex Edmonds
Series editor: Alex Woolf
Designer: Victoria Webb
Map artwork: Peter Bull

First published in 1998 by
Wayland Publishers Limited, 61 Western Road
Hove, East Sussex BN3 1JD, England

Find Wayland on the internet at http://www.wayland.co.uk

Cover pictures: Ornamental hip mask (left), and Fulani fabric from Mali.

British Library Cataloguing in Publication Data
Sheehan, Sean, 1951–
Benin and other African Kingdoms. – (The ancient world)
1.Benin – Social life and customs – Juvenile literature
2.Africa – Social life and customs – Juvenile literature
I.Title II.Levy, Pat
966.8'3

ISBN 0 7502 2172 0

Printed and bound in Italy by
G. Canale & C.S.p.A., Turin

Picture acknowledgements: Robert Aberman 14; Ronald Sheridan, Ancient Art and Architecture Collection Ltd 17, 19, 35, 45; C.M.Dixon 27, 56; E.T.Archive 46 (British Museum, London); Getty Images 22–3, 28, 29, 36, 37, 42, 57; John and Penny Hubley 15, 49, 58; Royal Geographical Society, Cover right, 9 (John Evans Photography), 38 (Mike Foster), 43 (John Evans), 51 (Mike Foster), 59 (Chris Caldicott), 60 (Paula Holmes); Travel Ink 4–5 bottom (John Gray), 48; Werner Forman Archive Cover left, 1 (British Museum, London), 4 (Ghana National Museum), 7 (National Museum, Nigeria), 11 (Entwistle Gallery, London), 12 (Museum fur Volkerkunde, Berlin), 13 (British Museum, London), 18 (British Museum, London), 20 (British Museum, London), 21 (Entwistle Gallery, London), 25 (British Museum, London), 30 (British Museum, London), 31, 32 (British Museum, London), 33 (Museum fur Volkerkunde, Berlin), 34 (Museum fur Volkerkunde, Berlin), 39 (British Museum, London), 40 (British Museum, London), 41 (P. Goldman Collection), 44 (Entwistle Gallery, London), 47 (Benin City Museum), 50 (British Museum, London), 52 (Wallace Collection), 53 (British Museum, London), 54 (Sudan Archaeological Museum), 55 (British Museum, London).

Contents

CHAPTER 1

The First Kingdoms

The history of Africa is an astonishing story, and the rise and fall of the African kingdoms is just one part of this remarkable tale. Kingdoms arose in different parts of the African continent, starting in the north but also appearing in the west and far into the south. Their histories are usually unrelated, though sometimes the fall of one kingdom is linked with the rise of another, stronger, kingdom. Some are separated in time by 2,000 years, and in space by 5,000 kilometres or more. Other African states developed without the need for a king.

African kings were powerful and often fabulously rich because of their ability to control trade in valuable goods like gold or salt. Their kingdoms often became famous outside Africa and their kings sent ambassadors to foreign lands.

▲ These elaborate swords were made by a guild of specialists to signify the special status of the king. They were used only for royal ceremonies in the Asante kingdom.

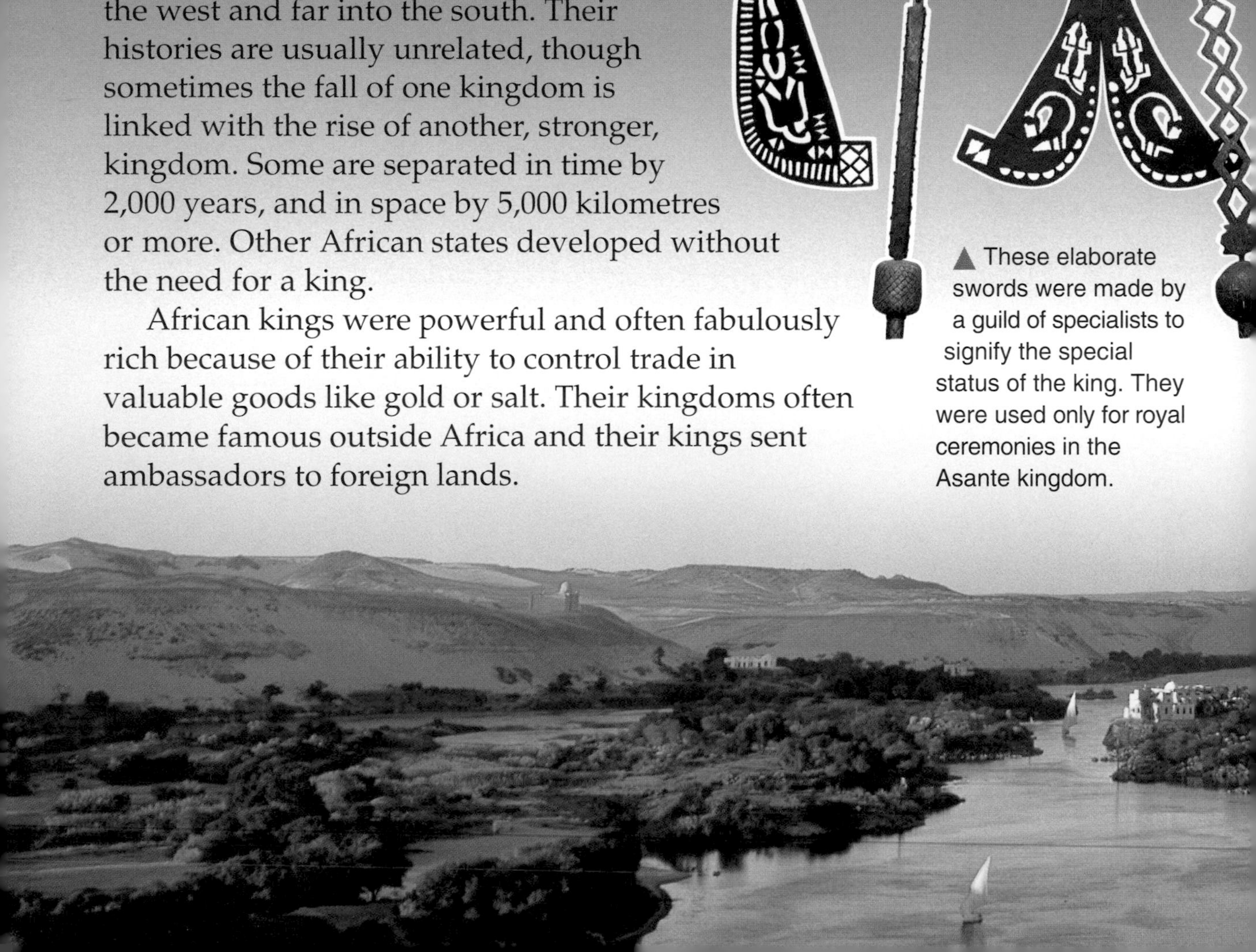

Most ordinary people lived their lives as farmers. Many of them paid a percentage of their produce to their rulers, and fought for them in the army. Although they had little more contact with their rulers than this, the beliefs and customs of the people of the African kingdoms were shared by all levels of society.

The history of African kingdoms began around 2500 BC, when what is now the Sahara desert was fertile land. As it slowly turned into a desert, the inhabitants drifted south into West Africa and eastwards to the River Nile. In the east the ancient Egyptians had already developed their majestic kingdom, but Egypt, though part of Africa, was unique. It is not known how or from where the idea of kingship developed. Perhaps, as agriculture evolved, leaders emerged who organized the planting, and gradually became very important to the community. Outside Egypt, the first African kingdom that we know of also developed close to the Nile: the kingdom of Kush.

One of the sources for historians of the African kingdoms are the oral histories that have been passed down from one generation to another. Professional storytellers recorded history by memorizing events. In the 1960s, one such storyteller in West Africa described why his work was important:

'…without us the names of kings would vanish into oblivion, we are the memory of mankind; by the spoken word we bring to life the deeds and exploits of kings for younger generations.'

▼ The River Nile flowed through the territories of the first two African kingdoms. It provided the Egyptians with fertile land to produce food, and enabled the Kushites to develop important trading links within Africa and around the Mediterranean. The town of Aswan, on the banks of the Nile, is shown here. It was, at different times, part of both ancient Egypt and Kush.

The Kingdom of Kush

The kingdom of Kush, in modern Sudan, lasted for over 1,000 years. It was Africa's first kingdom outside of Egypt. During the eighth and seventh centuries BC the rulers of Kush (also known as Nubia) governed Egypt as pharaohs, but around 666 BC they lost control over Egypt after being driven back by Assyrians from western Asia. Over the next 1,000 years 60 Kushite kings and queens governed Kush, but we do not know much about them. This is because the Kush language remains undeciphered, and much of what is known is based on archaeological evidence alone. The Kushites, who had challenged the power of ancient Egypt, were brilliant traders and are known for being the first people to use elephants for warfare and ceremonial occasions. There is even a building near Musawwarat which is thought to have been a stable and training centre for elephants.

The Kush kingdom was vast; stretching south from the border between Egypt and Sudan, along the River Nile for over 1,000 km. The positions of the borders to the east and west are not certain, but pictures of prisoners carved on Kushite monuments suggest frequent periods of warfare with nearby groups. In 24 BC, when Egypt was under Roman control, the Kushites attacked the Egyptian town of Aswan. The Romans then invaded Kush, but they withdrew because their troops were needed elsewhere.

▼ Meroe was the capital of the Kush kingdom from the seventh century onwards. It is possible that trade routes led from Kush to the lands of the River Niger in West Africa.

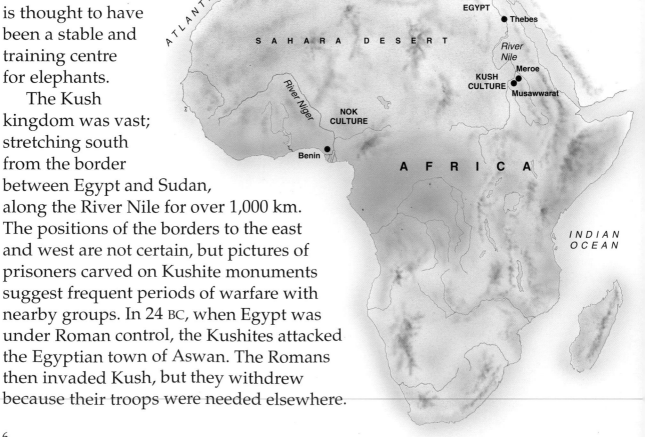

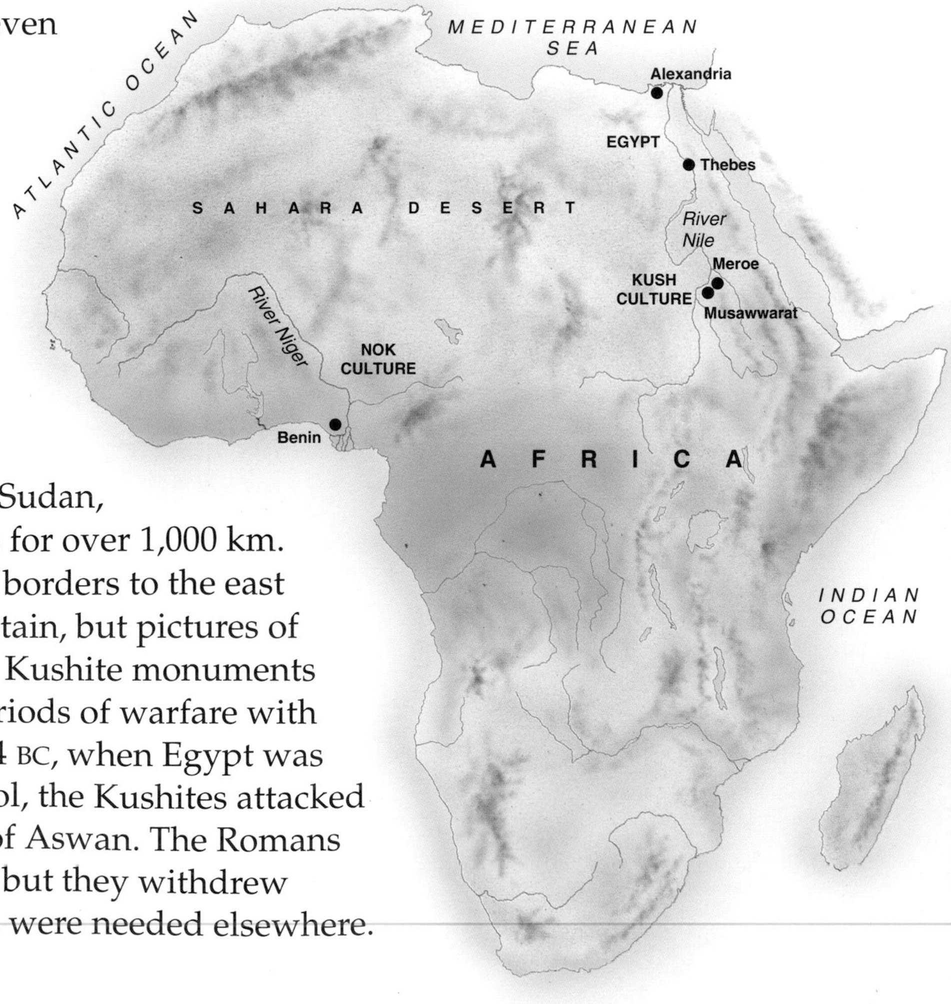

A gradual decline in Kush power is shown by the decreasing size and splendour of the tombs and pyramids built by the Kush; this happened from the first to the fourth centuries AD.

We don't know when or how the kingdom of Kush crumbled; but from around AD 250 the state slowly disappeared as it lost control over its territory.

Iron smelting was an important activity in the Kush capital of Meroe. It is possible that this is how knowledge of iron-making reached other parts of Africa.

On the other side of Africa, in what is now Nigeria, a society known as the Nok culture emerged some time around 500 BC. It declined, like Kush, around AD 250. The Nok were the first people south of the Sahara to practise iron-making, but we don't know where they gained this knowledge from. The carefully crafted clay sculptures of the Nok are evidence of an artistic culture; and the influence of their technology and art was felt in the early kingdoms that emerged in West Africa.

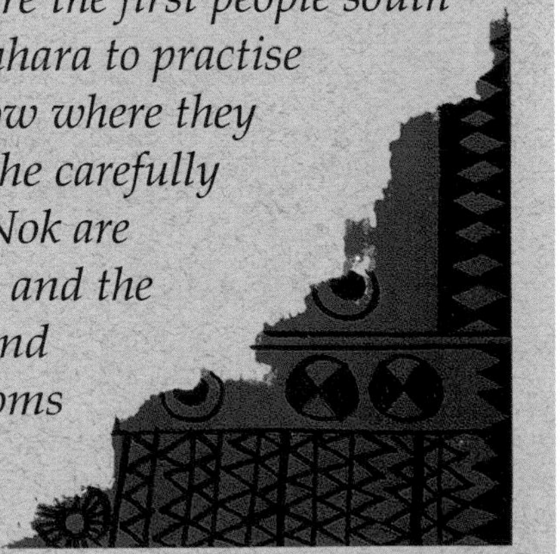

▲ This startling sculpture, in terracotta, or baked clay, belongs to the Nok culture. Such figures usually represented an ancestor and would have been placed in a family shrine.

CHAPTER 2

Ghana, Mali, Ife and Great Zimbabwe

Ancient Ghana

Ancient Ghana was the first well-documented kingdom in West Africa. The people of the kingdom were the Soninke, and their descendants still live in parts of West Africa today. Ancient Ghana was at its height around AD 750. Its astonishing wealth came from collecting taxes on the trade of gold and much-needed salt. The gold lay to the south of ancient Ghana and it had to pass through the kingdom before being traded for salt. The Muslim merchants transported this salt across the Sahara desert from the north of Africa. Ghana was therefore able to impose taxes on both the gold producers and the Muslim traders, and in this way its powerful rulers grew tremendously rich. Ghana also had a large, well-equipped army to protect its people and its riches.

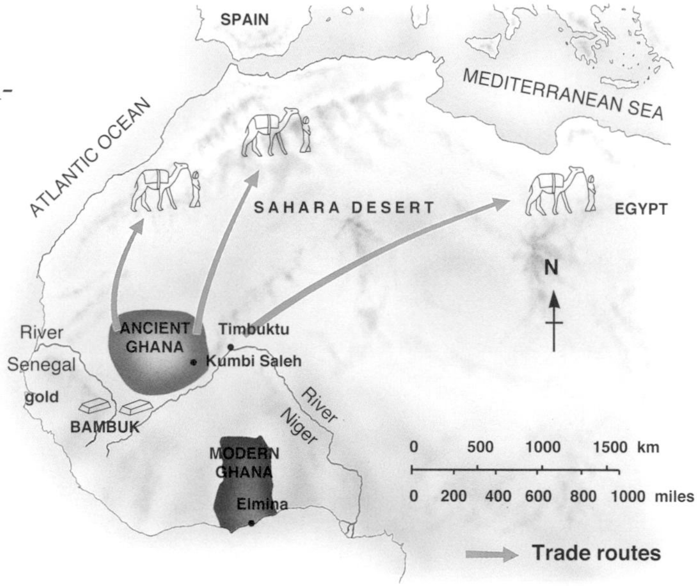

▲ The name 'Ghana' was the title of the king of the region. It is not the same as modern Ghana, which lies to the south-east of ancient Ghana.

The capital city of the kingdom was Kumbi Saleh. It was discovered by archaeologists in 1941. It was a large city with a population of around 20,000. The kingdom of ancient Ghana lasted for over 300 years and was eventually conquered by a group of Muslims from North Africa known as the Almoravids.

The Almoravids mounted a campaign against Ghana in AD 1070, but it took over six years to finally defeat the kingdom's army and then capture Kumbi Saleh. The Soninke people eventually regained some independence and established a new capital. However, Ghana never regained its power because the gold supply to the south of its kingdom ran out. Early in the thirteenth century the power of ancient Ghana was finally overcome by the rise of the new kingdom of Mali.

Most of what is known about ancient Ghana comes from Muslim historians. Al-Bakri, an Arabic historian in Spain, published his *Book of the Roads and Kingdoms* in AD 1068. He did not actually visit Ghana, but based his account on the reports of traders and travellers who did.

This extract, from al-Bakri's account, shows the King of Mali's wealth. It also shows how the kings kept the sons of local rulers as hostages:
'He [the king] sits in a domed pavilion around which stand ten horses covered with gold-embroidered cloths. Behind him stand ten pages holding shields and swords decorated with gold; and on his right are the sons of vassal kings of his country, wearing splendid garments with gold plaited into their hair. At the door of the pavilion are dogs of an excellent breed… round their necks they wear collars of gold and silver.'

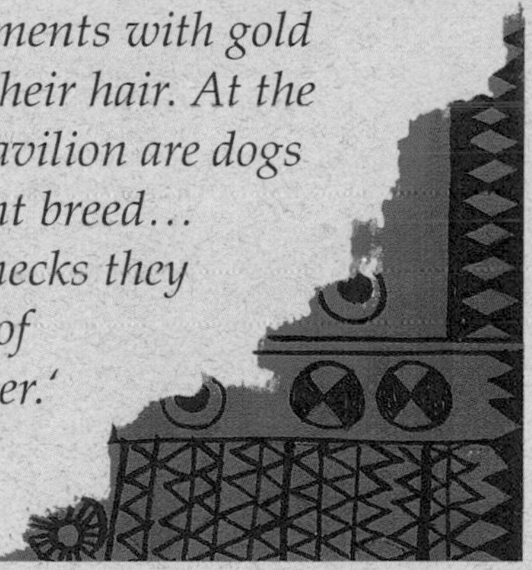

▼ Modern caravans follow a trading route dating back to the eleventh century.

Mali

As the kingdom of Ghana declined, there was a struggle between various groups to take control of the valuable gold trade. Sundiata, a local king, emerged as the victor, and he laid the foundations for the kingdom of Mali in the early thirteenth century. Mali was able to control a new source of gold along the River Niger. The kingdom also expanded eastwards to include Timbuktu. Muslim merchants made Timbuktu an important town for the Saharan trade routes. In time the ruling class of Mali was converted to Islam. The king of Mali had the title Mansa, and the most famous Mali rulers were Mansa Musa and Mansa Suleyman; they ruled in the first half of the fourteenth century. Mansa Musa made a famous pilgrimage to Mecca. He made the year-long trip a chance to show off his legendary wealth. It is said that he carried with him over 1,000 kg of gold and that his most important wife had 500 maids and slaves to accompany her on her journey. After Mansa Suleyman died, in 1360, there were disputes over who should rule. Many of the succeeding kings were either weak or oppressive. By 1400 the kingdom began to break up: first, the rich city of Gao broke away; then the Tuareg people of the southern Sahara invaded the north of Mali and captured Timbuktu. There was still a Mansa in the seventeenth century, but the kingdom had shrunk drastically; the glorious era when the Mansa was a strong force in Africa was long gone.

▼ At its height, the kingdom of Mali stretched eastwards from the Atlantic for 2,000 km; and 1,000 km from north to south. It included all the territory of the older kingdom of Ghana. Gold sources were found close to the River Niger.

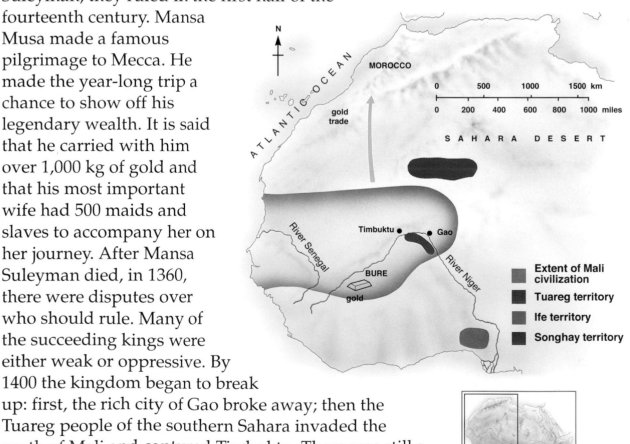

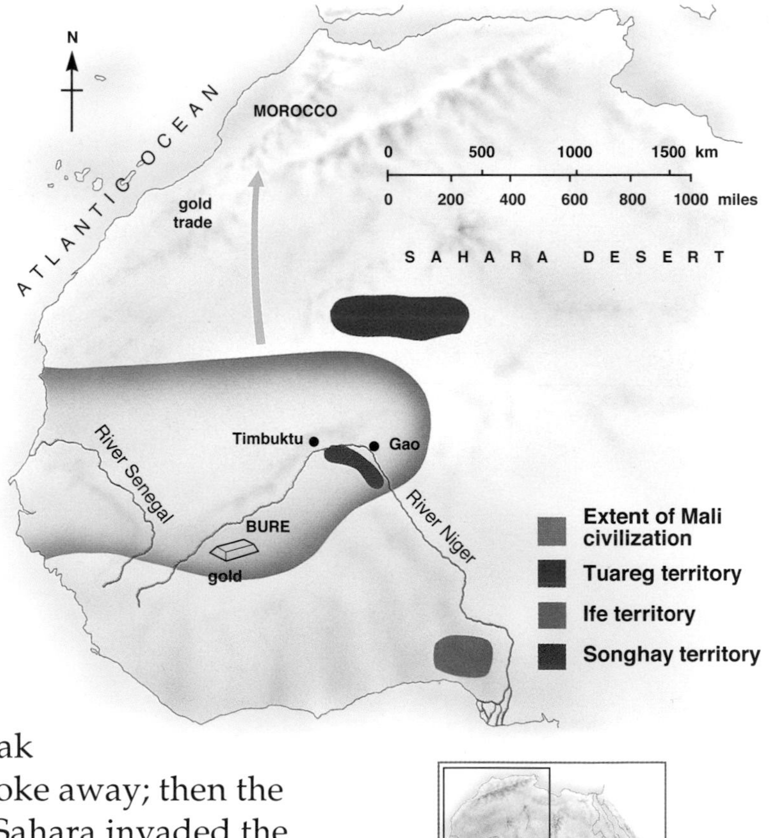

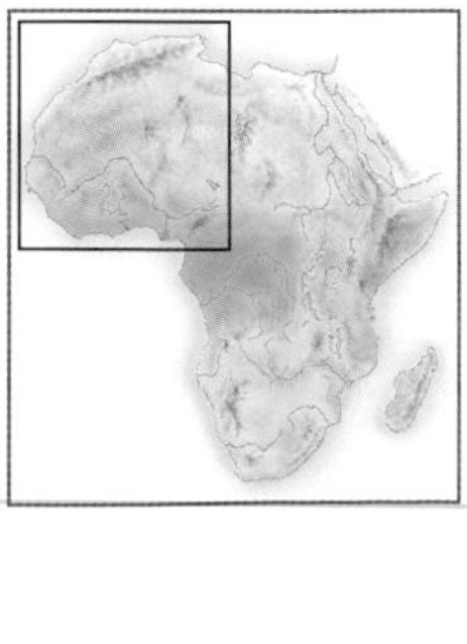

As with ancient Ghana, most of what is known about the Mali kingdom comes from Arab historians. They wrote their accounts in the fourteenth century, based on oral traditions and histories they had collected from travellers. One of them, Ibn Battuta, visited Mali during the reign of Suleyman. He was very impressed by the kingdom: 'They are seldom unjust, and have a greater dislike of injustice than any other people… There is complete security in their country. Neither traveller nor inhabitant in it has anything to fear from robbers or men of violence.'

◀ This strange figure of a seated man resting his arms comes from ancient Mali. His body is encircled by a snake. The function of this terracotta figure is unknown.

As the Mali kingdom declined, it was succeeded by the kingdom of Songhay, based along the River Niger. The Songhay people lived close to the Niger and they were master canoeists. The greatest Songhay king was Sonni Ali the Great, who became king in 1464. He was famed for his magical powers. A Muslim writer noted that during the 27 years of his reign, 'When he [Sonni Ali] was present, none of his armies was defeated.' After his death, the kingdom survived for another hundred years until it was overthrown by an army from Morocco; but at its height Songhay controlled more territory than even Mali.

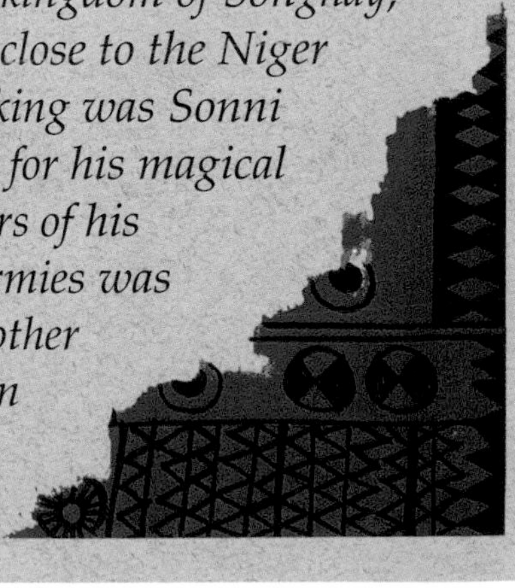

Ife

The Ife kingdom of the Yoruba people (see map on page 10) was one of the earliest kingdoms to emerge in the West African rain forest, some time around AD 600. The story of Ife begins around 200 years earlier, when the Yoruba people first occupied the rain forest. They knew how to make iron tools, and this technology allowed them to clear huge areas of forest land. This had previously been impossible to clear because people only had stone and bone tools. Gradually, over the next two centuries, villages developed and chiefs emerged from the powerful families. Ife became the holy city of the Yoruba and its ruler, the Oni, was king of all Yoruba kings. The first king was Oduduwa, and one story relates how he descended from heaven on a chain. Another legend says that he was a prince who came from afar; this may refer to the arrival of a new group who gained enough control to rule over the original settlers.

◀ The sculptor of this terracotta head from Ife has captured the features of his subject's head and face with remarkable skill.

A German scholar, Leo Frobenius, was the first to discover Ife pottery. In 1910 he found, 'one or two bits of reddish terracotta embedded in the earth... They were pieces of a broken human face... Here were the remains of a very ancient and fine type of art... [with] a vitality, a delicacy of form directly reminiscent of ancient Greece'. Frobenius mistakenly thought the ancient Greeks must have had a colony in West Africa, because, like many Europeans at that time, he could not believe that 'backward' Africa could produce such beautiful art, or that it could have created such a sophisticated society.

The discovery of very beautiful terracotta, copper and brass figures from Ife provides an important source of information for historians. The pottery dates from the twelfth to the fourteenth centuries, and the brass and copper figures from the fourteenth and fifteenth centuries. They are intricate, lifelike sculptures, and making them required great skill. To the people of Ife, art was a method of expressing religious devotion and a way of worshipping their gods. Copper – which is also contained in brass – was not available locally, so it is likely that the kingdom developed links with the trade routes that crossed the Sahara to get these materials. The Ife probably learned their iron-working and pottery techniques from the Nok culture.

By the sixteenth century, Ife had declined in importance, but the role of the Yoruba people continued with the kingdoms of Benin and Oyo.

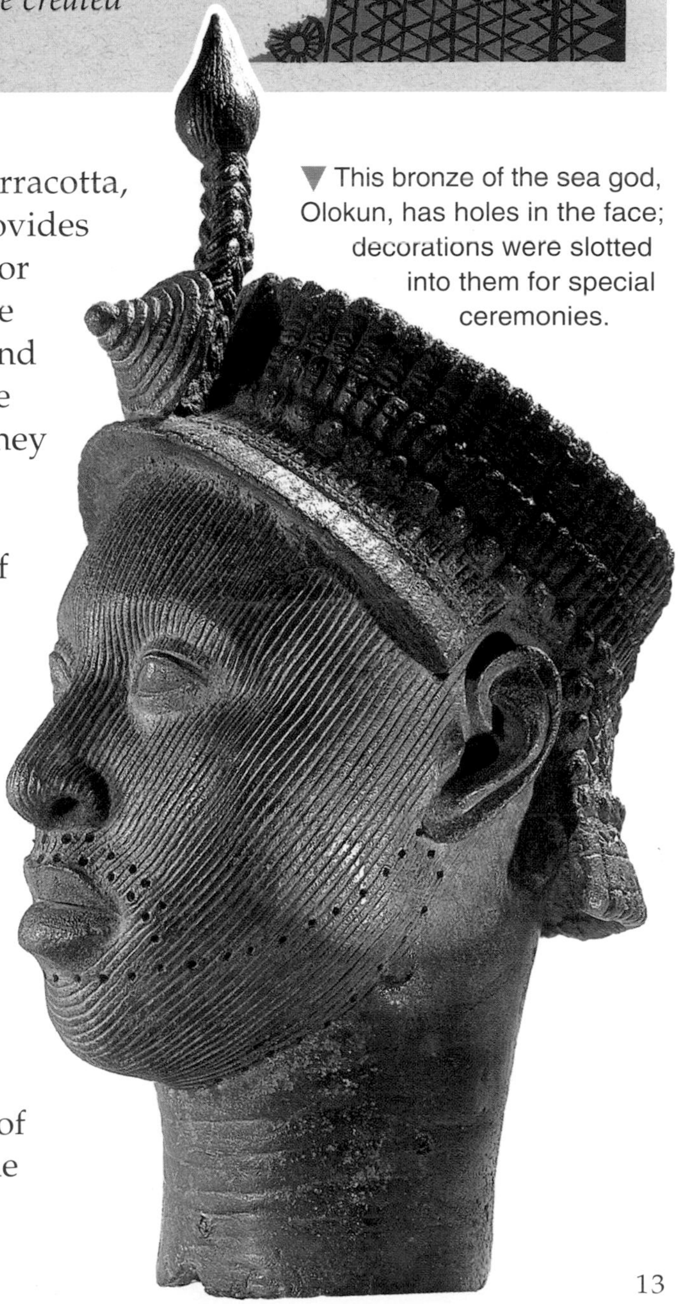

▼ This bronze of the sea god, Olokun, has holes in the face; decorations were slotted into them for special ceremonies.

Great Zimbabwe

Around AD 1000, the powerful kingdom of the Shona people emerged in the south of Africa. The Shona were one branch of the Bantu people. Bantu-speaking people probably spread into the south of Africa from a region in West Africa, around the first century AD. The Shona kingdom is named after their word for a royal court, a *zimbabwe*. The largest of their palaces, called Great Zimbabwe, is the biggest and most important building constructed in southern Africa before modern times.

▼ Great Zimbabwe was on a trade route to the coast, as we see from this map. The map also shows the location of the stone ruins of Great Zimbabwe and some of the smaller zimbabwes built by local rulers.

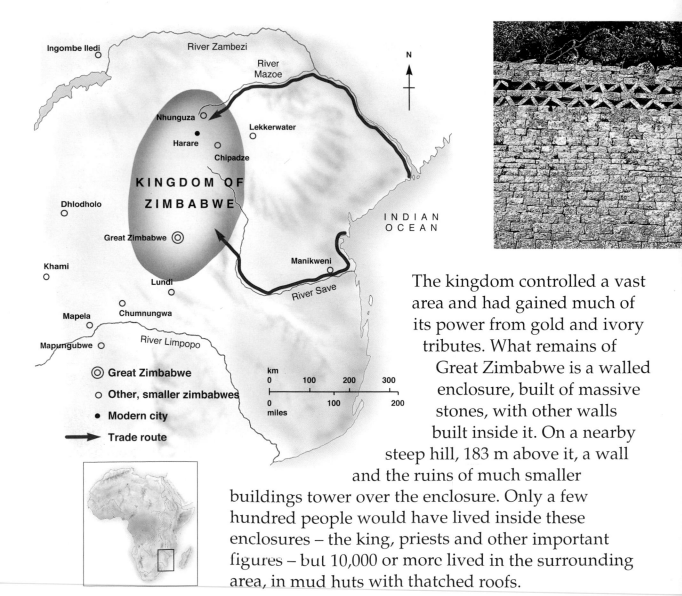

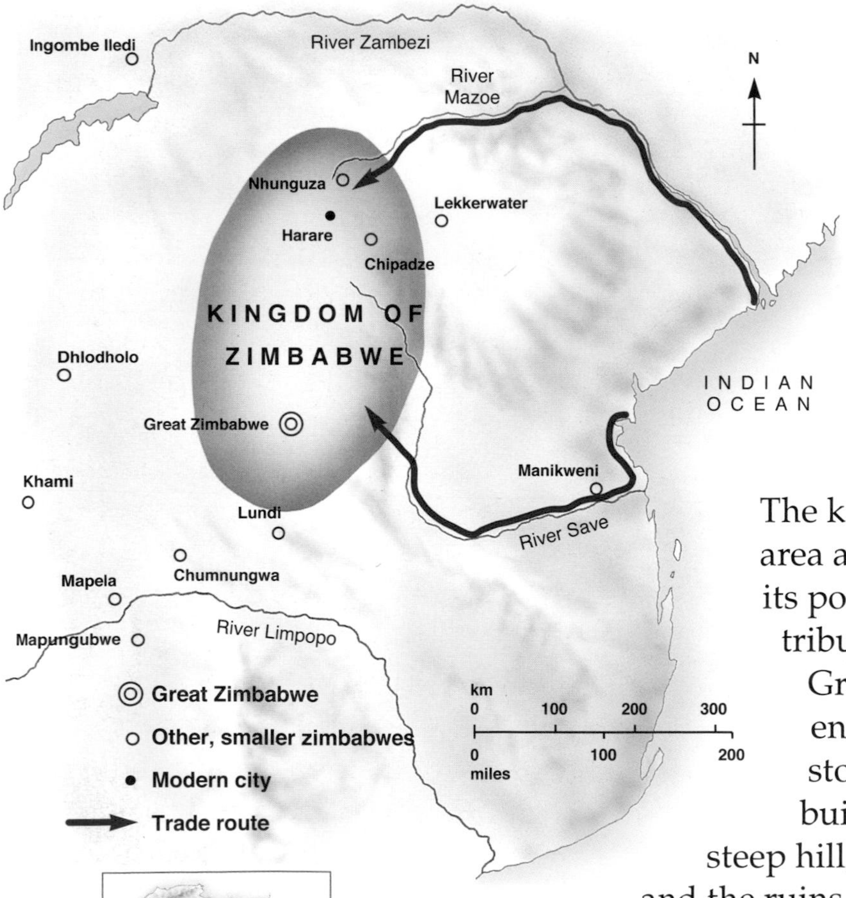

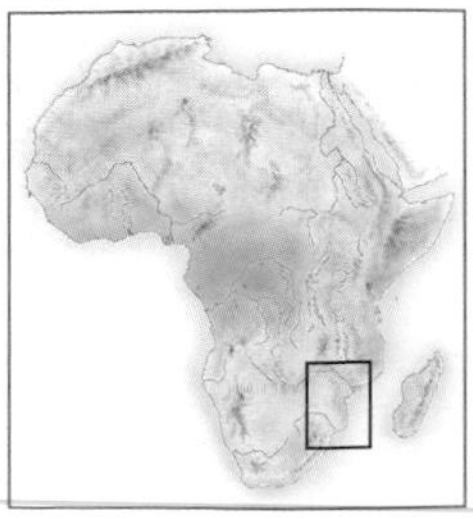

The kingdom controlled a vast area and had gained much of its power from gold and ivory tributes. What remains of Great Zimbabwe is a walled enclosure, built of massive stones, with other walls built inside it. On a nearby steep hill, 183 m above it, a wall and the ruins of much smaller buildings tower over the enclosure. Only a few hundred people would have lived inside these enclosures – the king, priests and other important figures – but 10,000 or more lived in the surrounding area, in mud huts with thatched roofs.

◀▲ The walls of Great Zimbabwe were over 10 m high and over 5 m thick, and had drains laid through them. The slightly sloping effect was created by setting each course of stones a little back from the one below. The Shona of modern Zimbabwe are the descendants of the people of Great Zimbabwe.

Modern archaeologists of Great Zimbabwe face problems that were caused by early European explorers. Some explorers were inexperienced and a lot of damage was caused to the site. Theft was also a problem; one group formed The Ancient Ruins Company, to sell their plunder. Even so, many artefacts have been saved: tools for smelting gold, copper and iron; instruments for making fine jewellery; and imported goods from India and China. Evidence of cotton-spinning and weaving has also been found.

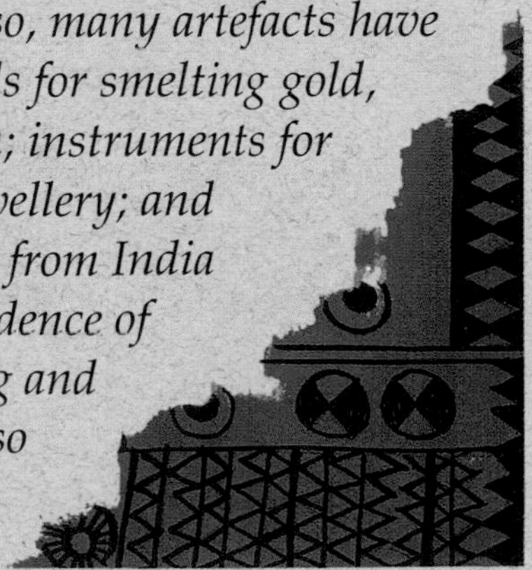

There were other independent states and smaller local kings and governors; altogether some 200 zimbabwes have been found in this part of southern Africa.

The nineteenth-century Europeans who explored Great Zimbabwe couldn't accept that Africans could have built such a magnificent palace. They said that King Soloman or the Queen of Sheba must have built it. Most of the treasures found were stolen by early visitors.

Great Zimbabwe was at the height of its power during the thirteenth and fourteenth centuries. Its wealth and power came from its control of cattle herds, and foreign trade through East African trade cities. In the late fifteenth century the kingdom was in decline, mainly due to the rise of the stronger Mwenemutapa dynasty to the north.

CHAPTER 3

Benin – the Forest Kingdom

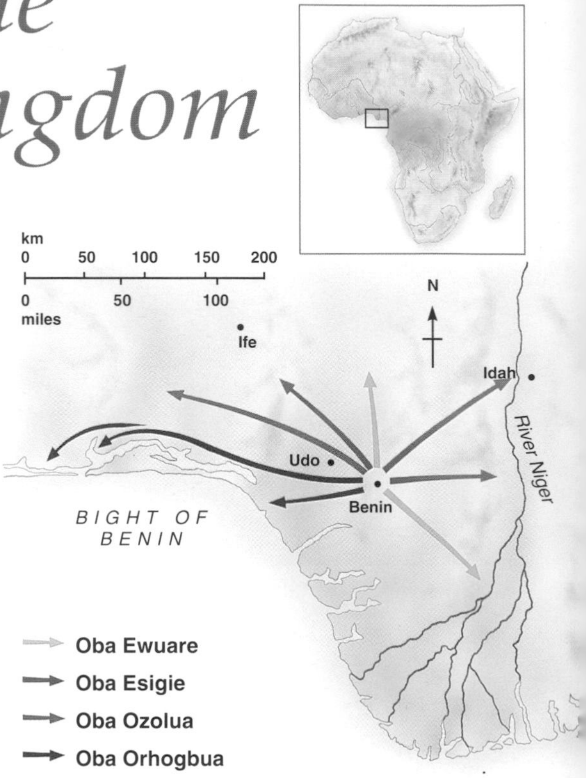

▲ The expansion of Benin is shown on this map. The four directional arrows show the expansion of territory under each of the first four warrior kings. Benin itself was a walled city of about 1.5 km square, and in the surrounding countryside there were other, smaller, walled communities.

Ewuare the Great

The Edo people, who live to the south-east of Ife, have a tradition that a prince from Ife established a new kingdom in the city of Benin. By the fifteenth century this kingdom of Benin began to expand under a series of five great warrior kings. The first of these kings was Ewuare the Great.

There are many tales of Ewuare's adventures before he became oba (king) around AD 1440. To become king he had to defeat many rivals and he is even said to have burnt down Benin to revenge his banishment from the kingdom by his predecessor. Once he was king he rebuilt the ruined city, with his palace at the centre. He became known as Ewuare the Great after he had built up a strong army and set about expanding his kingdom. He is said to have captured over 200 towns, commanded the construction of good roads and built a defensive wall around Benin. His people believed that he was a great magician, physician, traveller and warrior. Under each of the wall's nine gates he laid magical charms.

Oba Ewuare made changes to the government to strengthen his kingdom. He decreed that his son would inherit the throne; he also created a council of five town chiefs to advise him on government matters and was involved in developing a strict legal system.

The palace of Oba Ewuare was run by three associations of Palace Chiefs, whose jobs included looking after the oba's family and managing the palace. Oba Ewuare established royal ceremonies and traditions that made the king the most important person next to the gods themselves. He also encouraged arts like ivory and wood-carving. He married his daughters to local chiefs to reduce the chances of a rebellion within local regions. Under Ewuare the Great the kingdom of Benin took the first steps towards becoming the most advanced, and most important, kingdom in West Africa.

◀ The horseman may be Oranmiyan, a thirteenth-century oba who is credited with having introduced horses into Benin. Such a figure would have been placed on an altar dedicated to ancestors.

A traditional tale about Ewuare records how, one morning, he saw a leopard on a tree: 'He got up hurriedly and then saw that he had been lying on a snake in the night. He killed both the leopard and the snake... vowing that if ever he should become Oba of Benin he would make it a place for worshipping the gods of his destiny. This vow he fulfilled... every year of his reign he sacrificed a leopard, and his example was followed by his successors.'

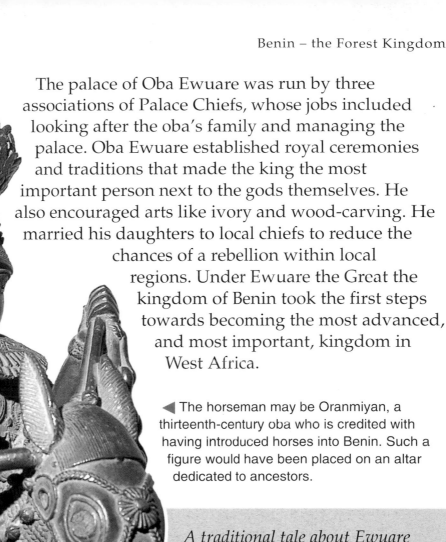

Warrior Kings

Oba Ewuare died around 1470, and the next four kings were all his descendants. Along with Ewuare, they are known as the Warrior Kings. Wars were common in Benin during this period; it is said that 100,000 warriors a day could be sent to war. Even if this is an exaggeration, it shows that their armies were huge.

Oba Ozolua came to the throne after his two older brothers had ruled for a short time; he was a more successful warrior than even his father, Oba Ewuare. The size of the Benin kingdom grew larger under Oba Ozolua, but tradition records that he was assassinated by his troops because of his selfishness. He was succeeded by Oba Esigie who first had to defeat his step-brother, who also wanted to be king. The step-brother was the chief of Udo town and he wanted Udo to replace Benin as the kingdom's capital. Oba Esigie also increased the size of the kingdom, north-west into Yoruba land and eastwards as far as the River Niger. He built a separate palace for his mother about 5 km outside Benin; by tradition the Queen Mother never saw her son after he became oba.

Oba Esigie was succeeded by his son, Orhogbua; in his reign the size of the Benin kingdom reached its greatest. Oba Ehengbuda, the last of the warrior kings, had to stop rebellions across the kingdom.

The history of Benin in the fifteenth and sixteenth centuries under these kings is also a time of great artistic achievement.

▼ A brass head of a Benin king, with inlaid iron eyes. Coral beads, shown here in the beaded cap with dangling strings, and the high collar that reached to the shoulder, were important symbols of the king's status.

One of the most privileged groups in Benin were the hunters. Chosen from only the most talented boys, hunters had to complete a tough apprenticeship. They learned how to move quietly and quickly through the land, and how to survive without food. The best of these hunters were often promoted to become elephant hunters, which was very dangerous, and well-respected, work.

◀ A delicately carved ivory bracelet like this one could only be worn by an oba. The king, in a ceremonial dress of coral, is depicted as the god Olokun.

Oral tradition records how Oba Esigie killed the bird of bad omen in a war against the Idah people. When a certain bird's cry was heard, his soldiers wanted to retreat because the bird's call was thought to mean they were all going to be punished. The oba replied:
'No, let us continue to pursue the enemy up the bank of the Niger… Do not listen to the bird crying punishment… Rest assured that victory is ours. Good or bad omen, the victory depends on our skill.' Oba Esigie had the bird killed and his army went on to victory.

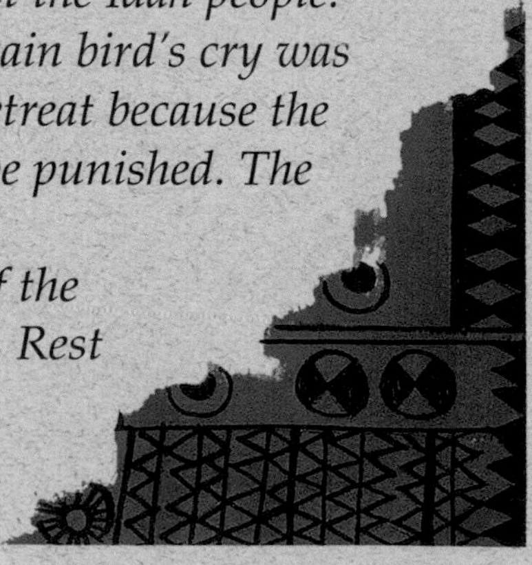

Contact with Europe

The Portuguese were the first Europeans to reach Benin, and a Portuguese historian wrote: 'This year, 1486, the land of Beny [Benin] was for the first time discovered… by Joham Affonso de Aveiro who died there.' The Portuguese were interested in trade, but they also helped Oba Esigie in his war against Idah. Benin was interested in buying items like coral beads, and the weapons of the Europeans.

In 1516 Portugal had its own ambassador in Benin and he wrote that the oba, 'sets us at table to eat with his son and no part of his court is hidden from us, but all doors are open.' Hoping for an easy profit, Portuguese traders were surprised at how sophisticated and business-like the officials of Benin were. The rulers of Benin saw the arrival of the Portuguese as a chance to increase their wealth and power in Africa. However, Portugal, driven by the huge demand for slave labour in the Americas, wanted more slaves than Benin would supply; and Portugal would not give weapons to non-Christian Benin. The relationship between the two countries deteriorated.

In the 1590s the Dutch came to Benin; they were very interested in trading for ivory. Throughout the seventeenth and early eighteenth centuries various Dutch, French and English traders all travelled to Benin.

◀ This ivory salt cellar was carved in Benin in the sixteenth century. The base shows two Portuguese noblemen with their attendants, while the top (the lid) is in the design of a ship.

Their accounts of their travels provide valuable information about life in Benin. Europeans were impressed by the splendour of Benin and even noticed and admired the thickness of the city walls. They wrote detailed descriptions of the palace. They noted the godlike status of the oba and the artwork being made for the palace. In the early seventeenth century Benin was at the height of its power and a Dutch reporter was very obviously impressed:

'The people have good laws and a well-organized police; who live on good terms with the Dutch and other foreigners... and who show them a thousand marks of friendship.'

The first slaves were taken from West Africa around the middle of the fifteenth century and taken to the Portuguese capital, Lisbon, where they were sold on. These slaves were treated the same as the white slaves in Europe; they were looked after because they were expensive. The European discovery of the Americas, however, changed everything. Now there was a huge demand for slaves to work in plantations in American colonies, and African rulers began trading people for fabrics and guns. Benin returned to trading slaves, this time with England.

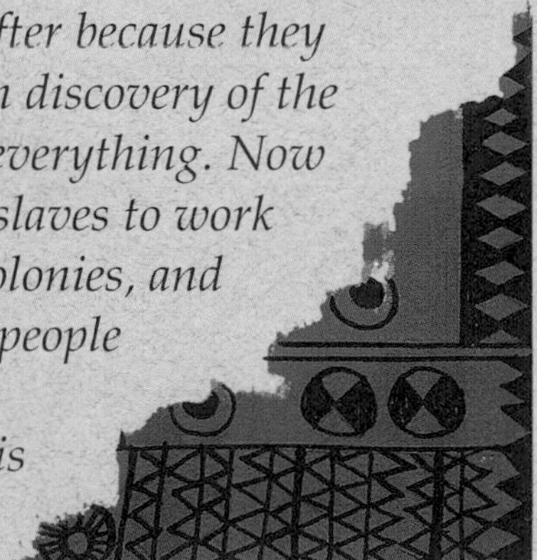

▲ This brass plaque, which adorned the oba's palace in Benin, shows two Portuguese males holding hands. The bearded man may be the father of the younger figure, while the details of dress suggest Benin's friendly curiosity about Europeans.

Decline and Fall

After the death of Oba Ehengbuda in 1606, Benin began to lose its grip on power. Ehengbuda's son became oba, but he died around 1640 without any heirs. There followed a period of civil war when rival rulers fought each other to establish control. It was not until the early eighteenth century that an oba ruled without opposition. However, the new period of peace and prosperity was not to last for long.

In the nineteenth century, a Yoruba kingdom from the west attacked Benin, and reclaimed most of Benin's Yoruba territory. Benin was growing weaker all the time. As its power slipped away, in desperation Benin began a period of mass human sacrifice, to appease the gods and their ancestors.

▼ A press photograph was taken of the captive Oba Ovonramwen, along with some of his chiefs, after the sack of Benin by the British in 1897. The British had the advantage of new automatic machine guns and many people were killed.

The British raided Benin in February 1897; they were there to revenge the killing of an Acting Consul General. The soldiers burnt down the homes of the important people of Benin, and the fire then spread to destroy most of the city. The palace was looted and one British official described what was stolen: '... in some of the houses were hundreds of bronze [brass] plaques of unique design; castings of wonderful detail, and a very large number of carved elephant's tusks of considerable age... there was a wonderful collection of ivory and bronze bracelets, splendid ivory leopards, bronze heads, beautifully carved wooden stools and boxes and many more articles too numerous to mention. A regular harvest of loot!'

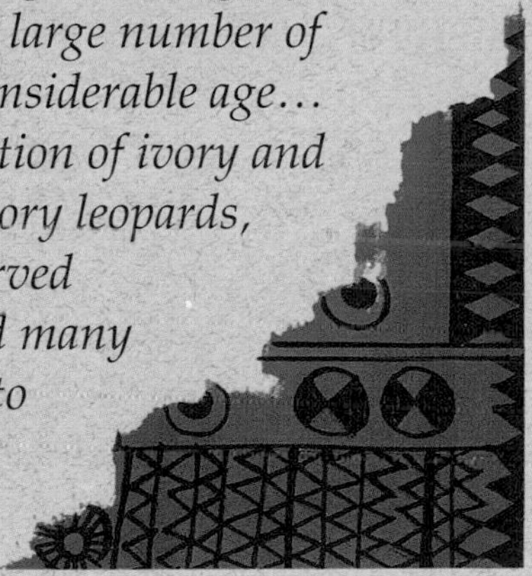

During the nineteenth century there was also conflict with the British, who wanted to control some of the trade belonging to Benin. In 1892 a trading treaty was signed between Benin and Britain. It is likely that Oba Ovonramwen did not fully understand the extent of the privileges that the British were gaining or how few benefits Benin was receiving from the treaty. In the years after the treaty, the oba stopped trading with the British many times.

Early in 1897, a British party of about 300 men, including traders and army officers, attempted to visit Benin. They were told they could not be seen because the oba was busy with a religious ceremony. The British went ahead anyway, but they were ambushed and seven of them were killed. In the same year the British returned with an army and captured Benin. Oba Ovonramwen was sent into exile and seven of his chiefs were executed. After the death of Oba Ovonramwen in 1914, his son was allowed to be crowned in Benin. The new oba's kingdom, however, was now part of British Nigeria. The independent kingdom of Benin, which had lasted for well over 500 years, was at an end.

CHAPTER 4

Later Kingdoms

▶ European visitors were astonished at the large number of gold ornaments, like this jewellery, worn by the chiefs and high-ranking officials of the Asante kingdom.

Asante

The Asante kingdom began to take shape towards the end of the seventeenth century. Before this, the Asante had been members of small states, each with their own chief. They came together under one Asantehene (King of the Asante), Osei Tutu, in around 1680.

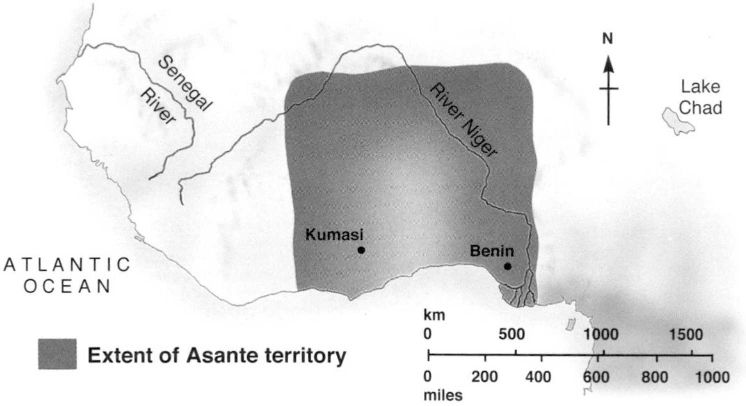

▲ The territory of the Asante kingdom is now part of modern Ghana. Kumasi, the capital, attracted European traders and merchants from all over West Africa, and Muslim scholars from Egypt.

Osei Tutu built up a strong army and began adding land to his kingdom by defeating local chiefs. The plan was to control important trade routes. Then, in 1765, one of Osei Tutu's successors added part of the coastland to the kingdom; and territory north of the rain forest was also attacked and taken over. The whole kingdom was governed from the capital in Kumasi. Asantehene Osei Kwadwo reorganized the army and made it more professional. He also created a police force and found officials to administer the kingdom and its provinces efficiently.

The Asante kingdom became very rich and powerful. It had its own supply of gold and, to add to this, provinces in the south paid their taxes in gold. It has been estimated that the equivalent of two billion dollars in gold was held in Kumasi.

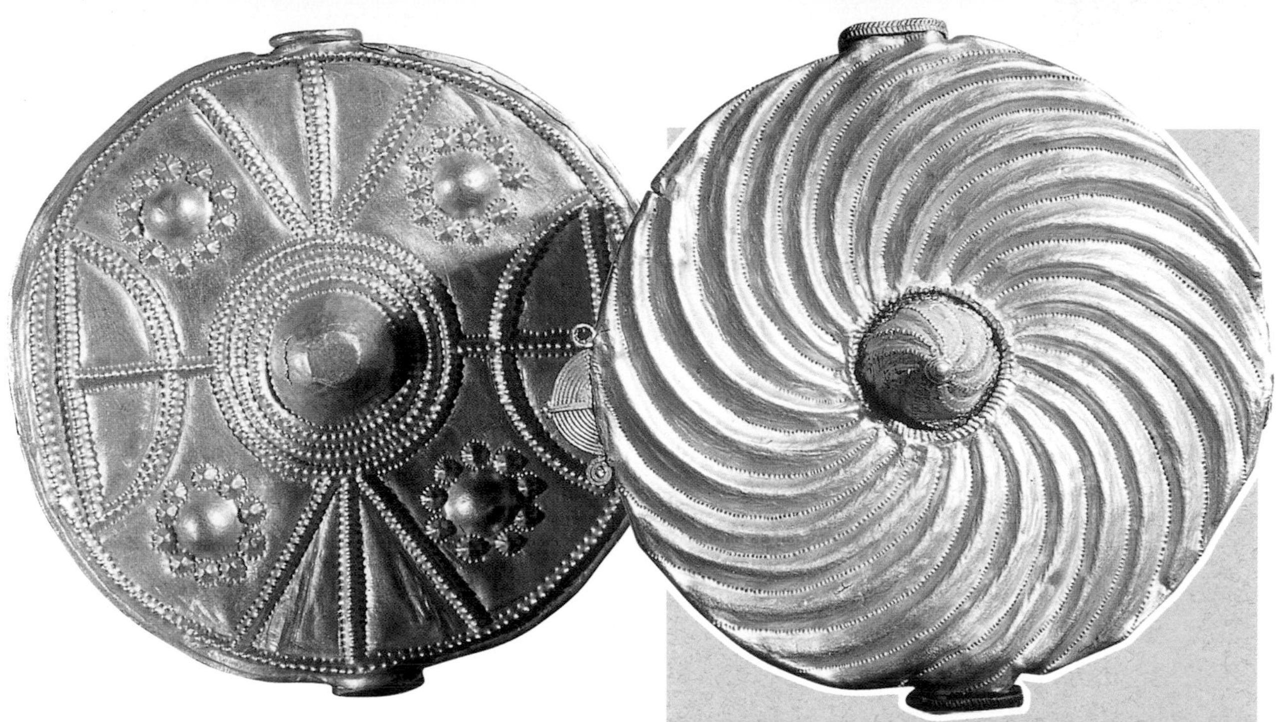

Provinces in the north paid their taxes in the form of slaves. The Asante then sold these slaves to European companies. The Asante successfully played Dutch and English slave traders off against each other, and developed their own slave trade.

The Asante were very artistic. Gold was used to produce works of art that helped to increase the prestige of the king and his ruling class. Leaders of the states under Asante control had to send their sons to the Asante court at Kumasi. There they were educated in the Asante culture, which they could then relay to their people.

Towards the end of the nineteenth century, conflict developed between the Asante and Britain. Britain wanted more control over the West African coast, to protect its valuable trade. Kumasi was sacked in 1874, and, after another defeat in 1900, the kingdom of Asante became a British colony.

When an Asante official took office, a spokesperson for the people was allowed a ritual request that the chief should be a fair leader:
'Tell him that we do not wish for greediness.
We do not wish that his ears should be hard of hearing.
We do not wish that he should call people fools.
We do not wish that he should act on his own initiative.
We do not wish that it should ever be said: "I have no time. I have no time."
We do not wish personal abuse.
We do not wish for personal violence.'

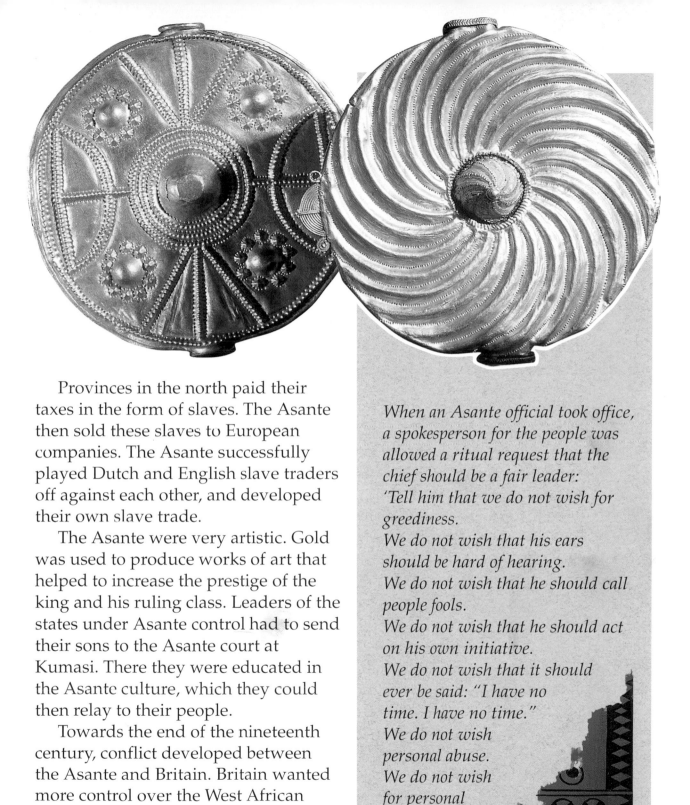

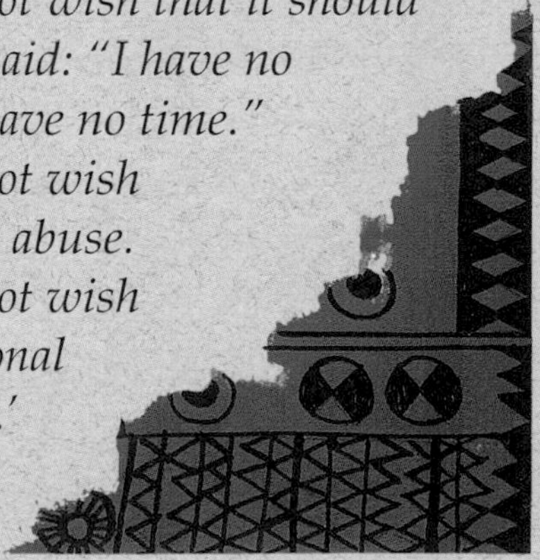

Oyo

Oyo was another Yoruba state, like Ife; and by the sixteenth century it was becoming the most powerful and culturally advanced kingdom in the land of the Yoruba. In the seventeenth century it conquered the neighbouring land of Ketu. After taking control of the River Ogun it had access to the coast, from where it traded with Europeans. Oyo also defeated the neighbouring land of Dahomey, and from 1730 onwards Dahomey had to pay Oyo an annual tribute.

Oyo's wealth came mainly from selling its war captives, as slaves, to the Europeans. Up to 20,000 slaves a year were being sold, in an area of Oyo's coastline that became known as the Slave Coast. Other sources of income were trade, farming and crafts.

Oyo's success depended on more than just wealth. It was a very stable kingdom and this had a lot to do with the way power was organized. There was a council of important chiefs, the Oyo Mesi, which advised the alafin (king) and passed laws. The Oyo Mesi decided who should rule after the death of an alafin. The crown nearly always passed to his eldest son. There was also a council of war chiefs, whose leader was known as the Bashorun. This council was in charge of the army. To prevent plotting against the alafin, on his death all of his officials and his eldest son had to kill themselves. But the alafin's power was not limitless; if the council of state and the people felt that he wasn't fulfilling his role they would present him with a dish of parrots eggs; this was a signal that the alafin should kill himself by drinking poison.

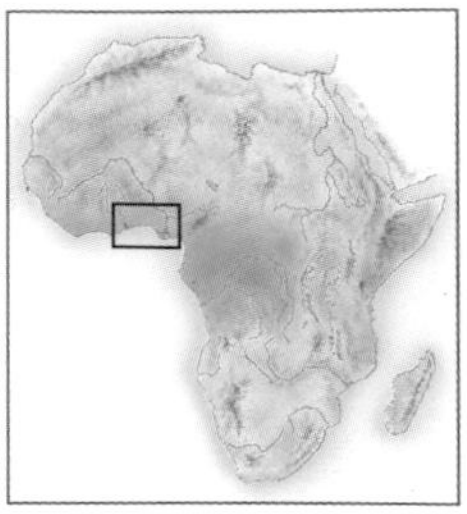

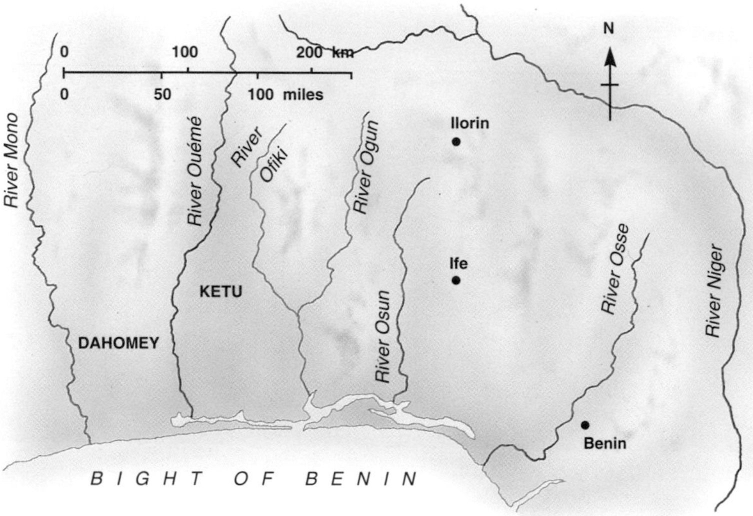

▲ With the help of a powerful cavalry and different types of swords, as well as spears with poisoned points, Oyo was able to considerably enlarge its territory. This map shows the Yoruba kingdom of Oyo at the height of its power.

▼ The metal loop at the top of this brass head was attached to a sash and worn at the hips by a Yoruba official at ceremonies. It symbolised the spirit of the chief's ancestor.

A British army officer travelled through Oyo in the 1820s. He noticed how honest the people were, and how even dogs were treated with respect:
'Here he had collars around his neck of different colours, and ornaments with cowries and sits by his master, and follows him in all his journeys and visits... In no other country of Africa, that I have been in, is this faithful animal treated with common humanity... I cannot omit bearing testimony to the... fact that we have already travelled 60 miles [100 km] in eight days... without losing so much as the value of a shilling...'

At the end of the eighteenth century, Oyo's power weakened. Some chiefs, who had grown rich by selling slaves, no longer accepted the leadership of the alafin. Fulani troops, who were Muslims fighting a 'holy war' for Islam, attacked Oyo. In 1835 the Fulani defeated Oyo at the battle of Ilorin. This was the end of the Oyo kingdom. A missionary, who visited Oyo in the 1850s, wrote of the battle:

'Within a few short days, that which was once powerful and flourishing, was now flowing with blood, covered with sackcloth, bathed in tears.'

The Zulu Kingdom

In southern Africa a powerful Zulu kingdom developed in the nineteenth century. Bantu-speaking people had travelled south, across the River Limpopo in AD 300; but it was not until the eighteenth century, after the introduction of maize, that the population rose. This led to rivalry between different groups, who competed for the good land necessary for farming and grazing animals. A king named Dingiswayo built up a strong group, and he was succeeded by Shaka of the Zulu clan around 1818. Shaka, who ruled for about 10 years, developed his Zulu army into a fierce war machine, and built up a strong kingdom. He attacked neighbouring land and added their cattle and soldiers to Zulu society.

European settlers all wanted good land in this part of southern Africa. The first conflict with the Zulu came from the Boers – Dutch colonists – but the British proved to be the biggest problem. Their empire was at its strongest in the second half of the nineteenth century, and the British were very interested in southern Africa. The Zulu, under their king, Cetshwayo, defeated an invading British army in 1879, at the battle of Isandhlwana. This, Britain's worst defeat in Africa, was followed by another defeat at Rorke's Drift. After this a new army was sent to defeat Cetshwayo.

▼ Cetshwayo, a nephew of Shaka, was 47 when he became the king of the Zulus in 1873, but when he first took part in raids against European settlers he was aged only 12.

▶ Cetshwayo was deposed by the British and sent to London after the defeat of the Zulus. Here he is seen leaving his country in 1879.

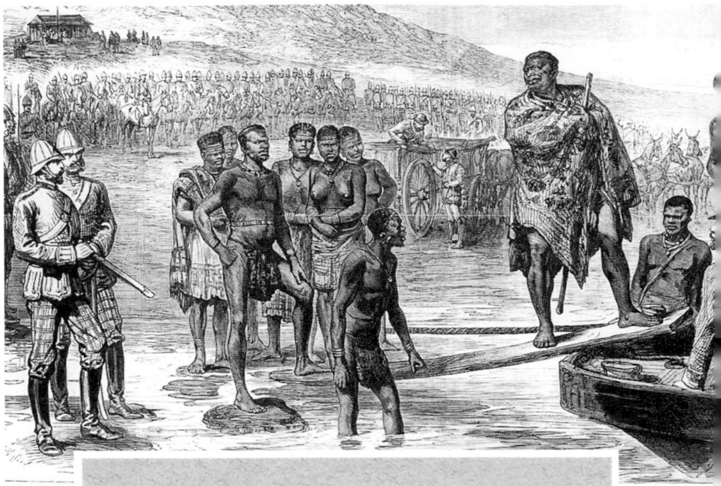

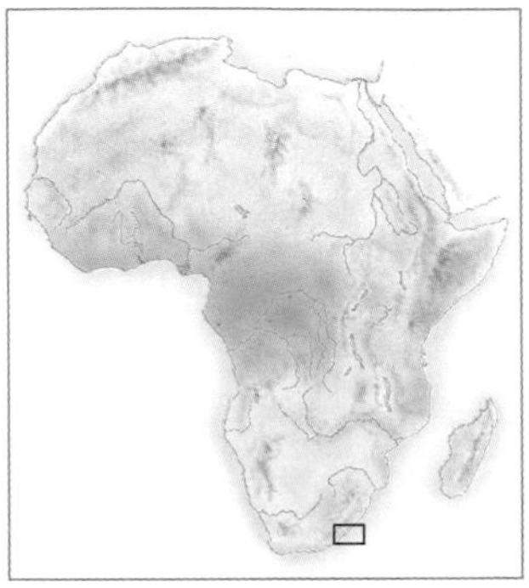

▼ The fertile land of the Zulu kingdom first attracted Dutch colonists, but it was the British who secured it for themselves.

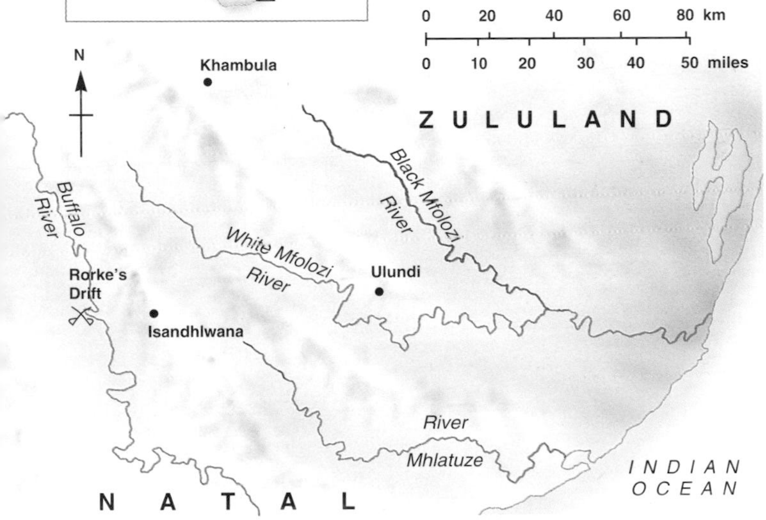

This time the British were better armed, and some 3,000 Zulu warriors were slaughtered by machine guns at the battle of Khambula in the same year – 1879. A final battle was fought at Ulundi, three months later. This time, more than 20,000 Zulu warriors were defeated by the rifles and machine guns of the British. The chiefs were then made to sign a document of surrender, the Zulu kingdom was split up into 13 separate districts under chiefs selected by the British and Cetshwayo was exiled and the Zulu kingdom was no more.

'I will observe and respect whatever boundaries shall be assigned to my territory by the British Government… I will not permit the existence of the Zulu military system… I will not import or allow to be imported into my territory… any arms or ammunition… In all cases of dispute in which British subjects are involved I will appeal to and abide by the decision of the British Resident… I will hold no trial and pass no sentence, except with the approval of such British Resident.'
From the terms of surrender signed by the 13 Zulu chiefs after defeat at Ulundi.

CHAPTER 5

Politics, War and Trade

The Drama of Royalty

Some African kings inspired huge displays of devotion. When a Kush or Oyo king died, it was customary for those close to him to commit suicide. Hundreds of years later, an Arabic traveller in ancient Ghana noted that: 'When people approach the king of Ghana, they fall on their knees and sprinkle their heads with dust.' The Mansa of Mali was so removed from his people that he did not talk to them; he communicated through a special messenger. The Oba of Benin had equally high status; people had to approach him on their knees.

▼ A pair of leopards, crafted in ivory with metal disks used for the spots and mirrors for the eyes. These would have been used for decorating either side of the throne, for royal ceremonies in Benin.

The oba's subjects could not look at him without his permission. Special adornments were usually associated with royalty. The oba, for example, was the only person who could wear a complete outfit of coral beads.

One reason for these customs was the air of mystery surrounding them; they helped to maintain the authority of kingship. Many African kingdoms also regarded their kings as godlike. The divine status of the Asante King was represented by a Golden Stool which was said to have descended from the sky '... in a black cloud and amidst rumblings.'

▲ In the Edo kingdom of Benin only senior chiefs could wear coral beads like the ones shown here, which were worn by a chief in 1964.

This is how a Muslim scholar described Mansa Suleyman, a fourteenth-century king of Mali:
'The sultan [king] presides in his palace on a great balcony where he has a huge seat of ebony that is like a throne fit for a large and tall person: on either side it is flanked by elephant tusks turned towards each other. His arms stand near him, being all of gold: sabre, lance, quiver, bow and arrows... As he takes his seat the drums, trumpets and bugles are sounded.'

A king was often regarded as the link between the spirit world of the gods and ancestors, and the people. The Asante had a weekly ceremony when the king asked the gods for forgiveness of his people's sins.

Having more than one wife was not uncommon in the African kingdoms, but no one could have more than the king. His many wives – up to 100 sometimes – would often come from different parts of the territory he ruled and this helped to unify the kingdom.

▼ This plaque may represent a court scene, with a warrior returning from battle with his guards, all heavily armed, accompanied by two musicians.

Court Life in African Kingdoms

The court was the centre of political life and the place where important decisions were made. It was a special group of buildings where the king lived and conducted the business of government. In the case of Great Zimbabwe, Benin and Oyo the court area was very large and surrounded by a wall; this was probably true of all the African kingdoms. Most ordinary people rarely saw those who lived inside the court because they were never allowed to enter. The people of Benin even believed that their oba did not need to eat or sleep.

Inside a large court there would have been plenty of activity. Governing a large territory involved meetings with local chiefs. Royal craftsmen often worked in special areas inside the court. Other rooms in the court were laid aside for rituals and shrines of ancestors; and the king and his various wives had their own living quarters. Staff and servants were always busy keeping the whole place in order. At every court there was also a host of resident officials, including priests, palace musicians and royal bodyguards. In the Oyo kingdom the officials who maintained the court were known as the Ilari. Men and women who became Ilari took a new name that honoured the alafin.

For example, one name translates into English as 'Do Not Oppose Him'.

Sometimes important members of the court had their residences outside the main court. From time to time there were power struggles within the court. One Bashorun, called Gaha, was noted for, '... having raised five kings to the throne, of whom he murdered four, and was himself murdered by the fifth.'

▶ This plaque adorned the walls of the oba's palace in Benin. The holes for holding it in place are clearly visible.

'The king's court is divided into many magnificent palaces, houses, and apartments of the courtiers, and comprises beautiful and long square galleries, about as large as the Exchange at Amsterdam, but one larger than another, resting on wooden pillars, from top to bottom covered with cast copper, on which are engraved the pictures of their war exploits and battles, and are kept very clean... Every roof is decorated with a small turret ending in a point, on which birds are standing, birds cast in copper with outspread wings, cleverly made after living models.'
From a description of the Benin court written by Olfert Dapper.

▼ Elmina Castle was built by the Portuguese in 1482, on the coast of West Africa, to extend and protect their African trade.

Trade

The success of the African kingdoms depended on their ability to trade. Each kingdom traded their rich resources for useful products that couldn't be produced locally, or for luxury items that would glamorize and increase the power of the royal court. The kingdom of Kush traded gold, ivory and slaves for wine, olive oil and ceramics from Egypt and the Mediterranean. The early West African kingdoms shared a trade in gold that crossed the Sahara to North Africa, and then on to Europe. Muslim merchants used ancient caravan routes across the Sahara; one caravan could involve more than 10,000 camels being led across the desert for up to three months.

In the fifteenth century the Portuguese explored the west coast of Africa and other European nations soon followed. They wanted gold – the basis for their own currencies – and peppers, to disguise the flavour of food that had been stored over the winter.

Ivory was also very popular. Benin was able to trade ivory in return for luxury items like coral beads, cloth, and brass.

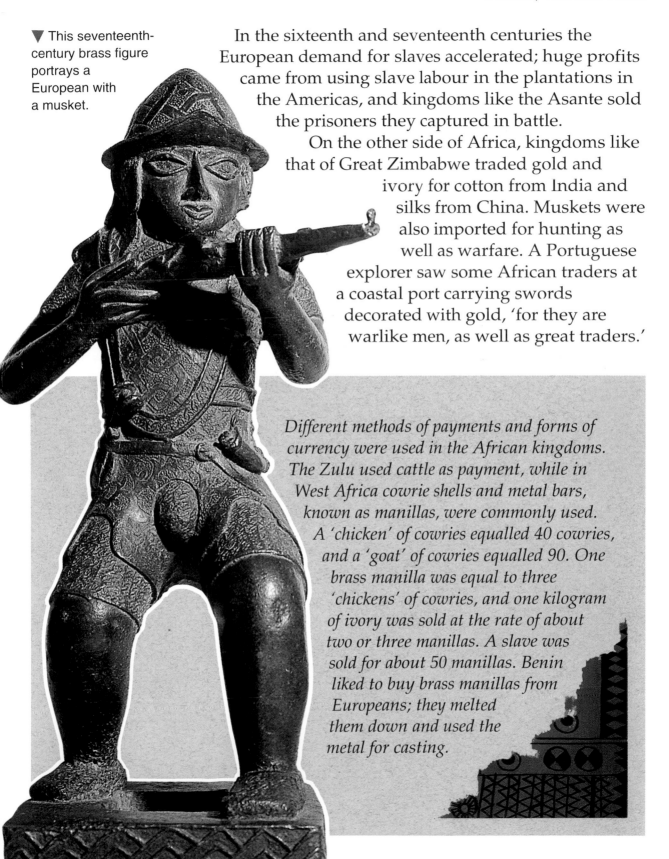

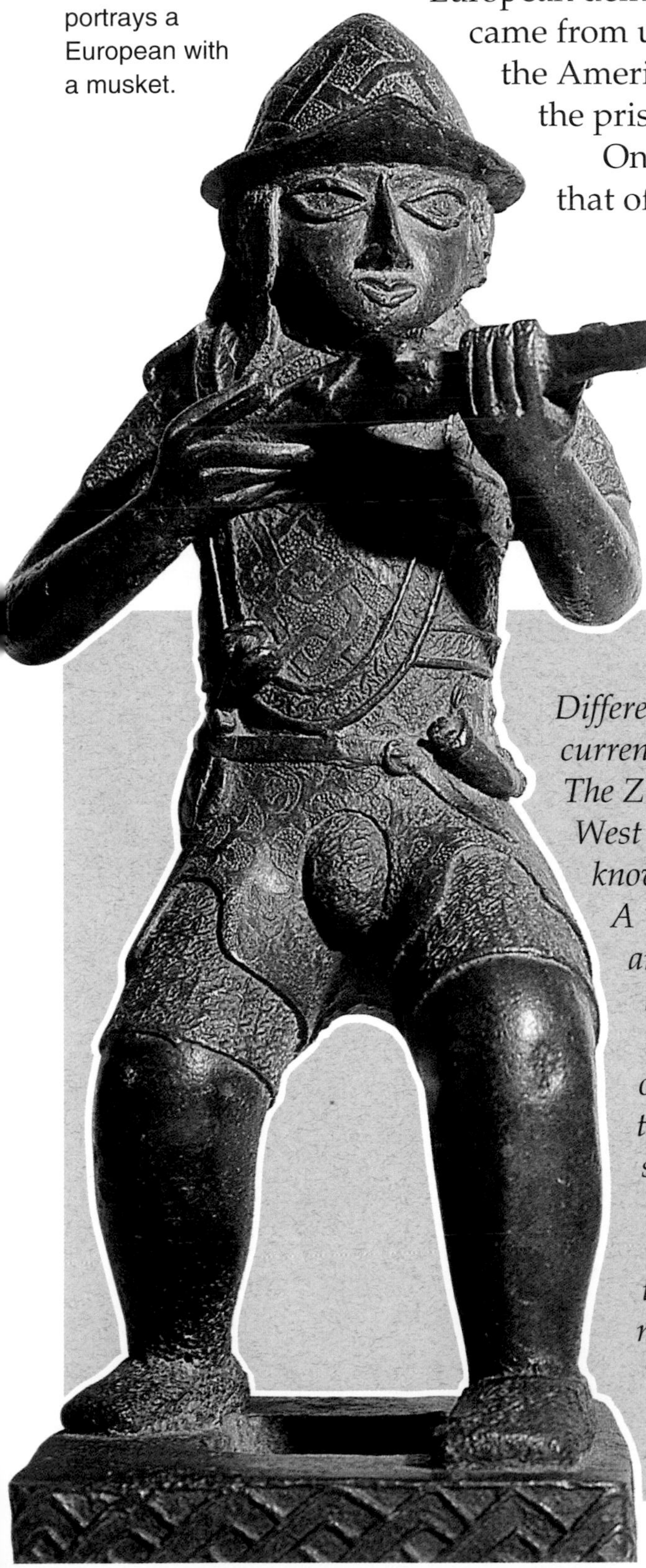

▼ This seventeenth-century brass figure portrays a European with a musket.

In the sixteenth and seventeenth centuries the European demand for slaves accelerated; huge profits came from using slave labour in the plantations in the Americas, and kingdoms like the Asante sold the prisoners they captured in battle.

On the other side of Africa, kingdoms like that of Great Zimbabwe traded gold and ivory for cotton from India and silks from China. Muskets were also imported for hunting as well as warfare. A Portuguese explorer saw some African traders at a coastal port carrying swords decorated with gold, 'for they are warlike men, as well as great traders.'

Different methods of payments and forms of currency were used in the African kingdoms. The Zulu used cattle as payment, while in West Africa cowrie shells and metal bars, known as manillas, were commonly used. A 'chicken' of cowries equalled 40 cowries, and a 'goat' of cowries equalled 90. One brass manilla was equal to three 'chickens' of cowries, and one kilogram of ivory was sold at the rate of about two or three manillas. A slave was sold for about 50 manillas. Benin liked to buy brass manillas from Europeans; they melted them down and used the metal for casting.

Arms and Armies

African kingdoms used a variety of weapons and armies in order to build up and defend their territories. The success of ancient Ghana was related to its knowledge of iron-making, which allowed it to produce iron-tipped spears and arrows – far superior to the weapons of stone, wood and bone used by its neighbours. The Songhay soldiers of Sonni Ali were reputed to take magic potions before going into battle, but their successes probably had more to do with a strong fleet of war canoes on the River Niger. When planning an attack on a city over 300 km from the river, Sonni Ali is said to have begun building a canal so that his navy could be used in the battle.

▲ Each Zulu regiment had its own intricate headgear and its own markings and colours for its shields. King Shaka was largely responsible for developing these regiments into a professional fighting force.

The ancient Greek historian, Herodotus, described how Kushite soldiers were: '... clothed in panthers' and lions' skins, and carried long bows... and on them they placed short arrows made of cane; instead of iron they were tipped with a stone, which was made sharp... Besides this they had javelins, and at the tip was an antelope horn, made sharp like a lance; they also had knotted clubs. When they were going into battle they smeared one half of their body with chalk, and the other half with red ochre.'

Oyo kings used some of their wealth to buy horses from traders to the north, and in this way built up a powerful cavalry. Oyo warriors, on foot or horseback, fought with spears tipped with poison. As a precaution against this, some soldiers fighting the Oyo had their front teeth extracted so that an antidote to the poison could be poured down their throats, despite their teeth being clenched in pain. European traders were often willing to trade firearms with West African kingdoms; by the eighteenth century about 200,000 muskets were being imported each year.

▼ Included amongst these Zulu weapons is the short spear, known as the *assegai*, introduced by King Shaka as a stabbing weapon for hand-to-hand fighting.

No warriors were more dedicated than those of the Zulu kingdom. Around the age of 18, all young men were enrolled into a regiment with their own barracks, uniform and herd of cattle. The cattle were carefully chosen to make sure their hides matched the pattern and colour of the regiment's uniform. The main weapons were a large cowhide shield, up to 1.5 m high and 1 m wide, and various spears. When attacking, the army used a 'beast's horns' manoeuvre: the centre, or 'chest', made a frontal attack, while the 'horns', made up of younger regiments, would swarm out to the sides to surround the enemy.

CHAPTER 6

Ideas and Religion

The Spirit World

The traditional African world of the spirits is a fascinating one, peopled by many different gods and goddesses, a host of spirits and a variety of supernatural powers. The everyday world of humans and the world of spirits are connected for the people of the African kingdoms. A strong link exists between the two worlds in African religion.

An important god for the Yoruba people of Ife and Oyo, as well as the Edo people of Benin, is Ogun. He is the god of blacksmiths, hunters, warriors and farmers, and is associated with the forging of metals. Strong weapons are also forged from metals and, not surprisingly, Ogun is also seen as a war god. The Edo believe that the god Osun is equally powerful; his spirit lives in the plants of the forest. Witchdoctors, called Ebo, can use the magical powers of certain plants to deal with the witches that may threaten humans at night. The Yoruba also feared Sango, the god of thunder, and his favourite wife, Oya, was the goddess of the River Niger.

▲ Any object, including this one in modern Benin, can become the focus for the belief in the world of magic and spirits. These objects are called fetishes.

For the Asante, the god of their main river was the most important deity, and the tributaries of the river belonged to the spirits of his wives and children.

The power of kings was often associated with the world of spirits. Sundiata, the early Mali king, presented himself to his people as a powerful keeper of magic and enchantment; and the kings of ancient Ghana lived close to the huts of the witchdoctors – probably for guidance and protection. The Asante had a weekly ritual whereby the Asantehene drank water from a gold vessel and spat it out, saying: 'Life for me – health for my people!' Kings who were seen as divine or semi-divine had the authority of religion to support them; anyone thinking of opposing them had to remember that they were challenging the might of both the gods and their mortal king.

▲ Almost all rituals in Benin involved sacrifices. This cow is about to be sacrificed; cows were regarded as the most worthy animal offering to the gods.

The Yoruba people had a very complicated system that priests used in order to divine what the gods knew about the future. A special divining board and 16 palm nuts were used to select a set of memorized verses that told a story. The priest had to memorize thousands of verses in order to perform the ceremony, and from the selected story the priest could advise someone about the future. The Bashorun of the Oyo had the privilege of being able to communicate with the spirit of the living alafin.

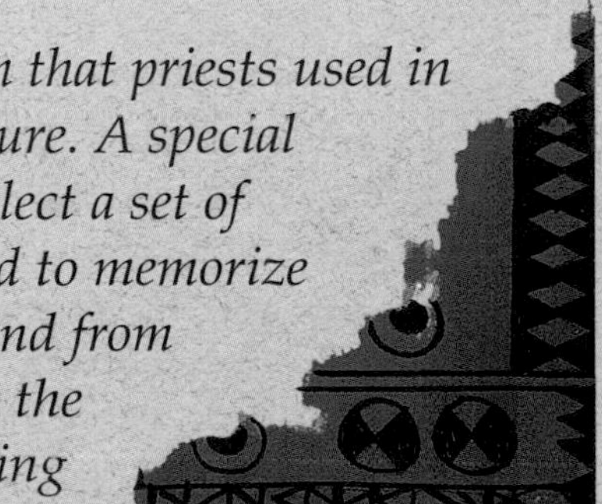

Ancestor Worship

Ancestor worship was common to most of the kingdoms we have looked at. It is a dramatic example of how traditional African religion brought together the everyday world and the world of the spirits. It was believed that ordinary people – as well as kings and chiefs – who lived a good life and earned respect, became ancestor spirits. They lived in the spirit world but watched over the living, and communication with them was possible. The most important spirit is that of a king, as his spirit is responsible for the continued well-being of the land.

It is possible that the hilltop ruins of Great Zimbabwe were home to a royal spirit medium who could communicate with ancestor spirits. Mediums communicated with ancestor spirits through the cries of a bird. Stone figures of a bird named Shiri ya Mwari, the Bird of God, were taken from the ruins by Europeans at the end of the nineteenth century.

In West African kingdoms, shrines and altars for ancestor worship formed a part of everyday life. In the palace at Benin there were 13 large courts, each of which had an altar for the ancestor worship of a past oba.

◀ This bronze figure, of an oba in ceremonial dress, adorned an ancestral altar in Benin. The loop above the head was probably for easy removal when the figure required polishing.

▲ The Yoruba believe that twins hold special spiritual powers. If one of them dies, twin figures like this were carefully looked after as a mark of respect to the spirit of the dead twin.

The decorations on the altars at Benin included brass commemorative heads, with ivory tusks resting on them. The ancestor altar of an ordinary home would have included wooden staffs, with a human head carved on the top, and a brass bell that would be rung at ceremonies. Usually only male ancestors were worshipped in Benin, but some kings and chiefs would have an ancestral altar for their mothers as well. One of the most important rituals in Benin was an act of ancestor worship carried out by the living oba; and before this ceremony took place all families in Benin celebrated the worship of their own ancestors.

A German traveller to Benin in 1603 provides the earliest known description of an ancestral altar in a home: 'They mourn their dead for three months, twice every day; and in the same house where the deceased father lies, the son who succeeds him has set up the heads of all the animals which his father has slaughtered and eaten – cows, goats, pigs, dogs, sheep, etc. – all around; it looks just like an altar. They also have large elephant tusks standing there, and all around they put as many wooden heads as the number of enemies whom the deceased father killed and slew in war during his lifetime.'

The Spread of Islam

The Muslim religion reached Egypt in AD 639, only seven years after the death of Muhammad, who had founded the new religion in Arabia. From Egypt, Islam spread across North Africa and reached West Africa by means of the caravan merchants crossing the Sahara. Muslim geographers gave the name Sudan – Arabic for 'the land of the black people' – to the new lands they found in West Africa.

The Soninke of ancient Ghana were the first group to make contact with Islam. Muslim warriors had made armed raids into this area, but peaceful trade soon developed as the best way of securing a regular supply of the precious gold. A Muslim settlement, for visiting traders, developed in the capital, but there was no attempt to convert the Soninke. In the eleventh century, the conquest of Mali by Muslims from northern Africa did impose Islam on local people, and when the kingdom of Mali replaced ancient Ghana, its rulers converted to Islam.

▼ Mecca, in modern Saudi Arabia, is the birthplace of Mohammed. Today, it remains the chief shrine for Muslim pilgrims from all over the world.

Mansa Musa made a pilgrimage to Mecca, the holy city of Islam, in 1324. This conversion became famous throughout the world of Islam.

Muslim teachers returned with Mansa Musa to Mali, and schools and law courts were established. New areas of learning, like mathematics, geography and medicine, were introduced. Reading and writing was learnt in order to study the Qur'an, and Timbuktu developed what would now be called a university. Scholars came to Timbuktu from all over the Islamic world, and much of what is known about the early African kingdoms comes from manuscripts written in Timbuktu.

▲ The mud-brick buildings of modern Timbuktu are similar to those that provided a home to Muslim scholars from the eleventh to the sixteenth centuries.

Kings like Mansa Musa and Songhay's Sonni Ali impressed Muslims by adopting their religion. The ordinary people, however, did not embrace Islam, and their kings had to be careful to still be seen as guardians of traditional African beliefs. Islam and traditional religions existed, peacefully, side by side.

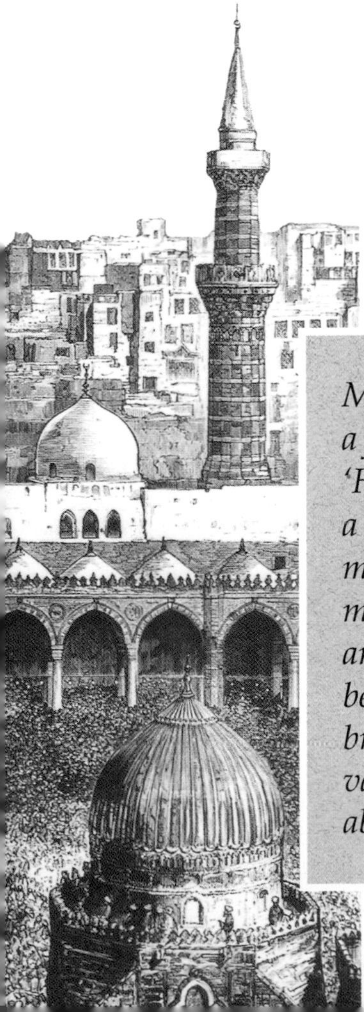

Mansa Musa's pilgrimage to Mecca stopped off in Egypt, and a fifteenth-century Arabic writer described his arrival: 'He was a young man with a brown skin, a pleasant face and a good figure… He appeared amongst his companions magnificently dressed and mounted, and surrounded by more than 10,000 of his subjects. He brought gifts and presents that amazed the eye with their beauty and splendour.' It is said that he brought so much gold with him that the value of Egyptian gold decreased by about 15 per cent as a result.

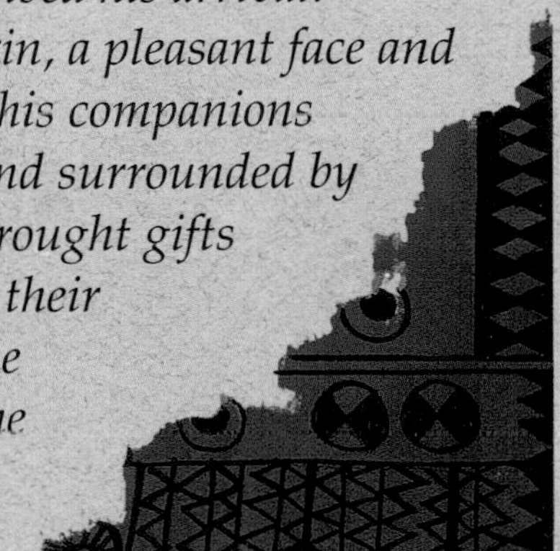

CHAPTER 7

Art, Architecture and Poetry

Art of the Kingdoms

Many objects that are now regarded as precious works of African art were commissioned by kings and chiefs. They were used in religious ceremonies, or to demonstrate the power and status of the ruler. Such work would rarely be seen by most ordinary people. Many other objects, now valued as art, were made for trade or as gifts. This would include pottery, textiles, tools and weapons.

Pottery was usually crafted by women, while sculpture in wood or metals was usually carried out by men. The earliest examples of West African sculpture date from the Nok culture. Their tradition of sculpture in clay influenced the art of Ife that followed centuries later. Asante art combines colour and design in rich textiles woven for men of high rank, and in the umbrellas made for state occasions. Much of the Asante kingdom's finest art was made by members of the privileged class of goldsmiths. A royal stool, ceremonial chairs and swords, and ornaments in the shapes of birds and animals were all crafted using gold.

▲ Nok sculptors were keen to portray faces with a sense of realism and attention to detail.

Lines of verse were composed to the gods, people, animals and even plants. The following is an example of the poetry of Praise Names. It is a Zulu praise of their king, Shaka:

'He is Shaka the unshakable,
Thunderer-while-sitting, son of Menzi.
He is the bird that preys on other birds,
The battle-axe that excels over other battle-axes.'

(English translation by Ezekiel Mphahlele)

Intricate jewellery – rings, necklaces, anklets and armlets – was made with gold leaf or cast gold. Zulu art, by comparison, often expresses itself in everyday objects like pots, plates and milkpails. However, elaborate carved wooden headrests were commissioned before a marriage, and brass jewellery was made for royalty.

Stone carvings and architecture are a feature of the cultures of both Kush and Great Zimbabwe. The Kushites constructed imposing temples, and their royal tombs symbolized the power of their kings. They built pyramids that were a lot smaller than Egyptian ones; they also built the tomb underneath the pyramid, not inside it. A Kushite pyramid that was discovered and robbed in 1834 contained all the jewellery of the queen, mostly made of gold and coloured glass.

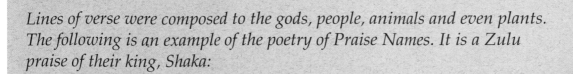

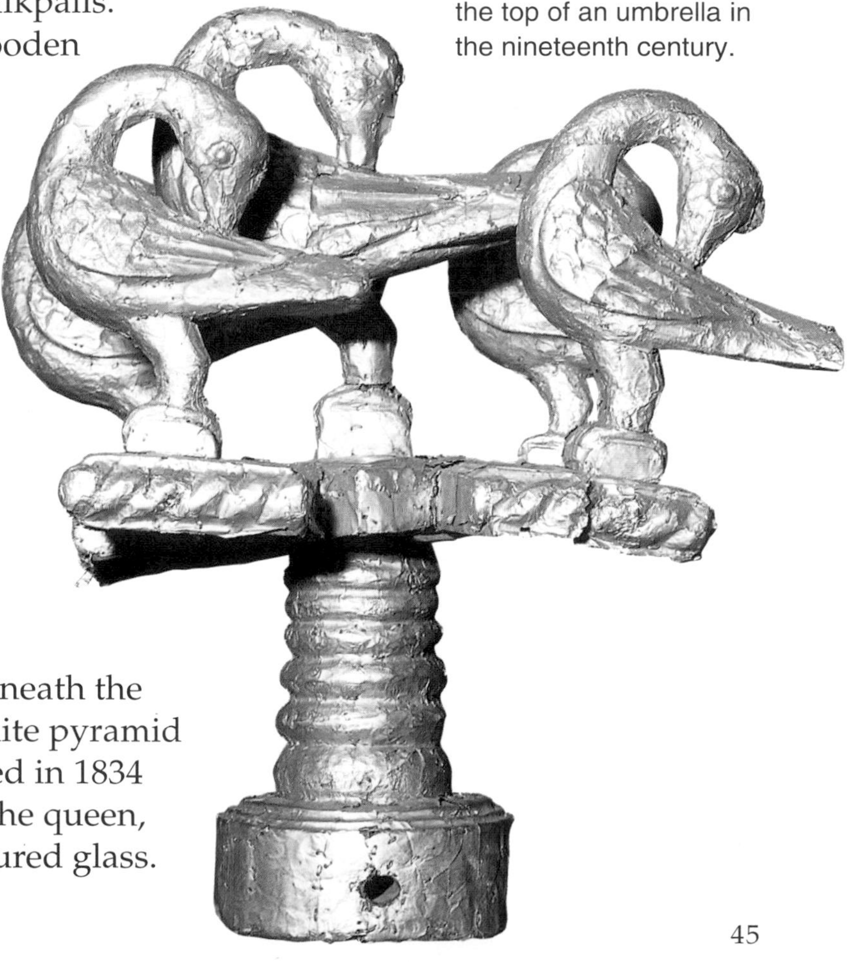

▼ Ceremonial umbrellas were part of the regalia of the Asantehene. These gold birds formed the top of an umbrella in the nineteenth century.

Benin Art

Benin art, which can be seen in galleries around the world, was a highly organized craft, under the control of the oba. Specialists in the different forms of art – brass-casting, wood-carving and ivory-carving – had separate areas of the court where they worked. They were organized into associations, or guilds, and in the case of brass-casters they were only allowed to work for the oba. Woodcarvers could work for other chiefs in the kingdom. Most of the craft specialists kept a workshop outside Benin, where they worked when there were no commissions from the oba.

The Benin tradition of sculpturing in brass, an alloy of copper and zinc, is said to have been introduced from Ife in the late thirteenth century. One of the finest art forms, developed by the Edo, was the crafting of rectangular plaques using brass. They were mounted, for decorative effect, on the pillars supporting the roof of the palace. The designs and pictures on the plaques, which stand out from the flat surface of the plaque, provide a lot of information about court life. Some of them record historical events and were probably commissioned for this reason. As we have seen, many of these plaques were taken away by the British, after their invasion in 1897.

▼ A prosperous and successful individual in Benin could erect a shrine to his hand – the source of his achievement and wealth. These shrines were usually carved in wood, but this one, made in the eighteenth century for an oba, was cast in brass.

Benin's artists also produced sculptures in ivory. Some of the most beautiful examples include carefully carved armlets, costume masks and other ornaments that were worn by royalty. Ceremonial iron swords and staffs, pendants, bowls and intricately carved tusks were also created for ancestor altars and religious rituals. Brass and ivory were the most sought after materials – they do not rust or rot. Ogun, the god of metal, was thought to have given brass the special power of bringing good luck; ivory was valued for its purity, and associated with another god, Olokun.

▲ This ivory pendant, showing an oba with two attendants, was worn on the hip as part of the oba's ceremonial dress.

The lost wax process is a method of sculpturing that was used in Benin to produce brass plaques. The basic shape of the figure is moulded in clay and covered with a layer of beeswax that can then be sculpted. More layers of clay are then applied and the whole model is heated until all the wax runs out through a specially made hole in the model. Hot brass is then poured in through the same hole. After drying, the original clay model is dug out from the figure, leaving the thin brass sculpture that formed where the wax had been applied.

CHAPTER 8

Everyday Life

Lifestyle

We have looked at the court life of African kingdoms, but the majority of people had little contact with this privileged world. For most people life was centred around their home, and their lifestyle was governed by their work. Most kingdoms had an urban capital; the Kushite capital of Meroe, for example, where about 20,000 people lived. Their average life expectancy was only about 20–25 years. The majority of people in all the kingdoms lived in, or close to, a village and earned their living as farmers. Kush settlements were usually close to the River Nile and many of the people in the West African kingdoms also lived close to a river. Some of the Kush were nomads who built and dismantled their tents or huts as they moved around to find suitable places to stay.

▼ Homes for ordinary people in ancient Kush would probably have looked very much like the ones photographed here, on the banks of the River Nile in the 1990s.

▶ Apart from the petrol station, this modern market in Benin would probably be recognizable to Europeans who traded with Benin centuries ago.

The local market was where people came together to buy and sell. The following description by a Dutch trader in Benin in 1602, gives an idea of what was available at a market: 'Much firewood and woodwork, such as dishes and drinking cups and other sorts are also brought to market for sale. Also much thread spun from cotton… They also bring a great quantity of ironwork to sell there, such as implements for fishing, ploughing and otherwise preparing the land. Similarly many weapons, such as javelins and others suitable for war and strife.'

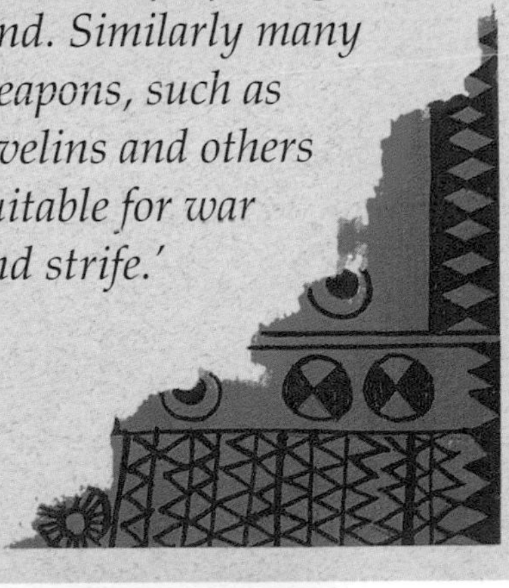

Mud, simply made from the dry soil and water, was used to build homes; the dried mud provided protection against most rainfalls.

If the climate was very dry, a flat mud roof and gutters were added. Otherwise, roofs could be made by overlapping large tree leaves until they formed a thatch. The living space in a Benin home was usually a low platform close to the walls, and there was also an unroofed courtyard area. The huts built close to Great Zimbabwe were made of *daga*, a durable form of cement, made by pounding the soil taken from ant-hills.

The homes of the wealthier people in Benin were described by a Dutch trader in 1602. He noted how the front door led to a small courtyard, covered with mats and kept clean by domestic slaves. An English trader wrote around the same time: 'They have good store of sope, and it smelleth like beaten violets… and spoones of Elephants teeth… with foules and beasts made upon them.'

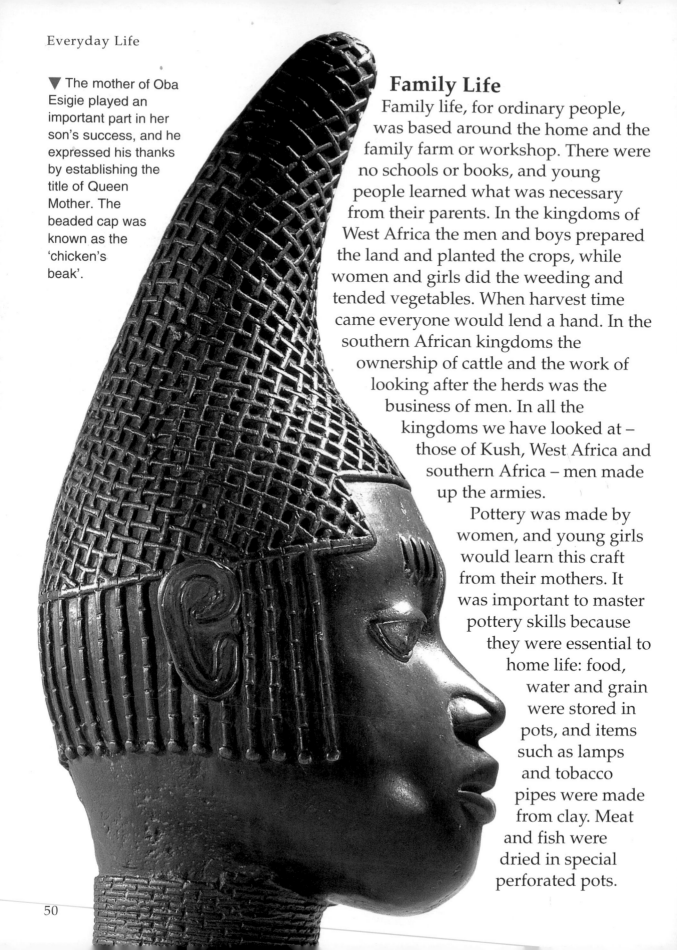

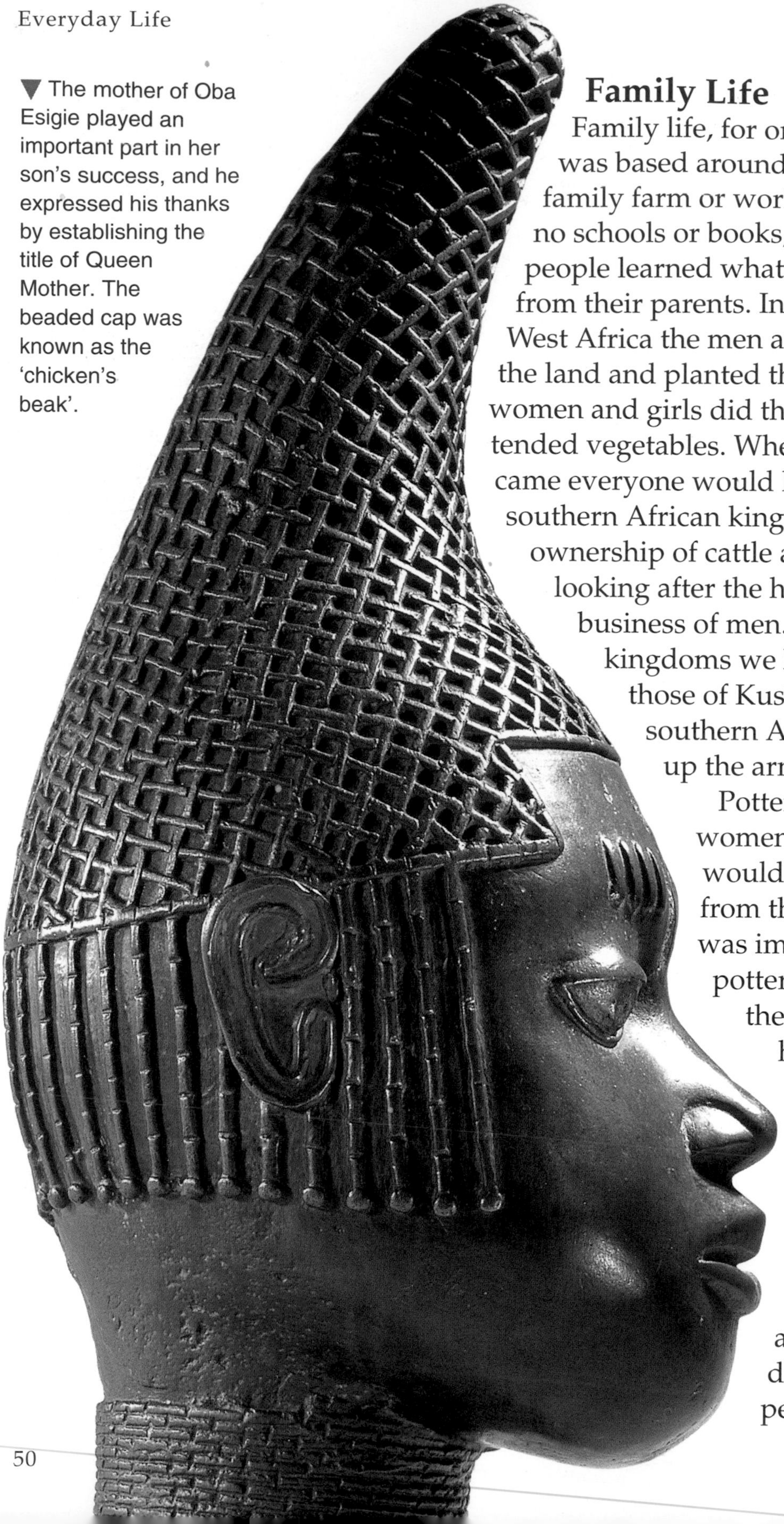

▼ The mother of Oba Esigie played an important part in her son's success, and he expressed his thanks by establishing the title of Queen Mother. The beaded cap was known as the 'chicken's beak'.

Family Life

Family life, for ordinary people, was based around the home and the family farm or workshop. There were no schools or books, and young people learned what was necessary from their parents. In the kingdoms of West Africa the men and boys prepared the land and planted the crops, while women and girls did the weeding and tended vegetables. When harvest time came everyone would lend a hand. In the southern African kingdoms the ownership of cattle and the work of looking after the herds was the business of men. In all the kingdoms we have looked at – those of Kush, West Africa and southern Africa – men made up the armies.

Pottery was made by women, and young girls would learn this craft from their mothers. It was important to master pottery skills because they were essential to home life: food, water and grain were stored in pots, and items such as lamps and tobacco pipes were made from clay. Meat and fish were dried in special perforated pots.

Family meals and other household affairs were the responsibility of women. Mothers would teach their daughters how to prepare food – using culinary skills such as pounding the grains of a crop like maize in a mortar and pestle. Cups and plates were usually made of wood, and pottery plates or dishes would be reserved for special feasts.

In Benin it was women who ran the markets, and this may also have been true of most of the other African kingdoms. One of Benin's female saints, Emotan, was a market trader who helped Ewuare before he became oba. An oral tradition tells how, after Emotan's death, Ewuare had a tree planted where she used to sit and sell her wares. In Benin, women were also musicians and storytellers, and it is likely that they could also own property.

▲ This woman in modern Zimbabwe has the responsibility for household affairs, just like countless generations of women before her.

In West Africa, rich families enjoyed far more variety in their food than ordinary families. Only the better-off would eat beef, mutton or chicken, and the majority of people depended on the crops and plants they grew themselves. Cereal crops like cassava, maize and sorghum were ground, and boiled water was added to the finely ground grains to make a porridge that was the staple food of the family. In kingdoms like Benin the staple food was yam (a starchy vegetable that looks like a potato) and it still is in many parts of West Africa. Poorer people also ate dried or smoked fish and plantain, a form of banana.

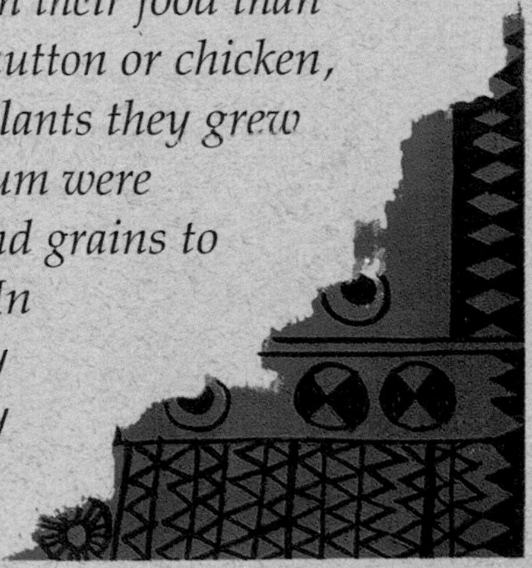

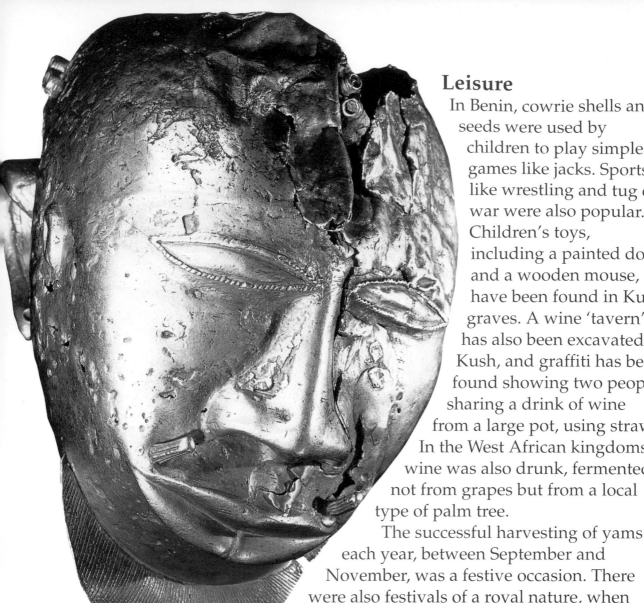

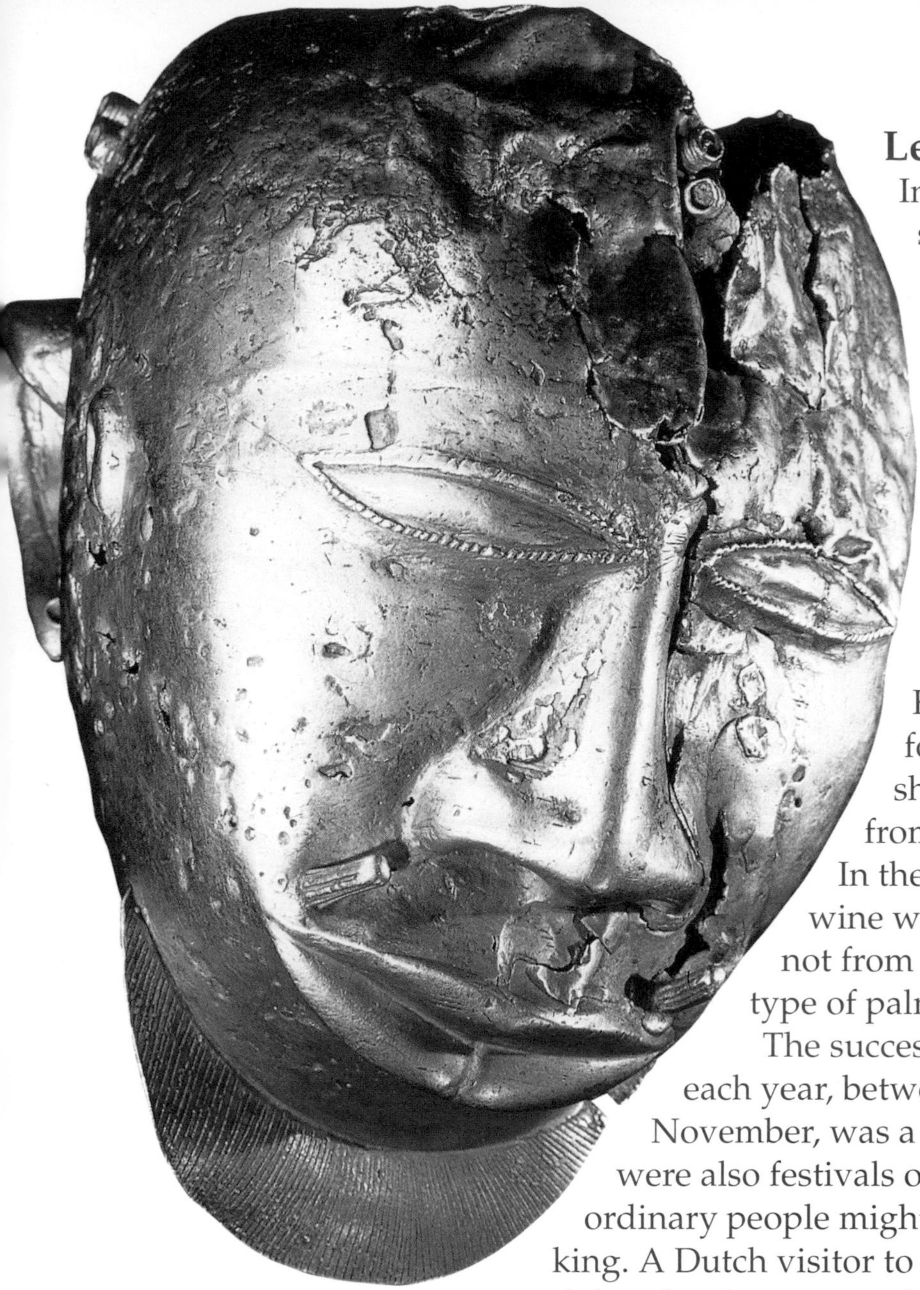

▲ An Asante goldsmith cast this head, representing an important enemy killed in battle, as an adornment to be added to the royal throne or a sword for use in ceremonies. It was later taken by the British after they looted the Asante capital in 1874.

Leisure

In Benin, cowrie shells and seeds were used by children to play simple games like jacks. Sports like wrestling and tug of war were also popular. Children's toys, including a painted doll and a wooden mouse, have been found in Kush graves. A wine 'tavern' has also been excavated in Kush, and graffiti has been found showing two people sharing a drink of wine from a large pot, using straws. In the West African kingdoms wine was also drunk, fermented not from grapes but from a local type of palm tree.

The successful harvesting of yams each year, between September and November, was a festive occasion. There were also festivals of a royal nature, when ordinary people might catch a glimpse of their king. A Dutch visitor to Benin shortly before 1600 noted that the oba appeared in public once a year: '… riding a horse adorned with ornaments, with a train of three or four hundred gentlemen, horses and cavalry, and musicians.'

On certain festival occasions the Asante carried their chiefs in public on open or covered chairs, richly decorated with colourful cloths.

The African kingdoms developed an amazing variety of musical instruments from simple materials. The hollowed-out, dried shells of the gourd plant were – and still are – used as amplifiers in different ways.

The art of storytelling, like the enjoyment of music, provided people with an inexpensive form of entertainment. A Benin historian, Jacob Egharevba, recorded this oral tradition of storytelling:
'When the day's work is done, they love to gather in groups in a neighbour's compound, to hear and tell stories. If the moon is shining the stories will continue well into the night.'
He also recorded how stories told by women, '... are usually interspersed by songs, with choruses in which all can join. The children soon pick up this kind of storytelling, and in their own way can do it as effectively as their elders.'

They could be hung under xylophones, or attached to a stringed bow instrument. Drums of all sizes and shapes were made from wood and covered with animal skin. Small hand-held pianos, known as 'thumb pianos', were made, using small metal or wooden strips attached to a sounding board. Percussion was often provided by metal bells, either singly or in pairs, fixed together. A variety of trumpets and flutes were also used.

▶ Live music, including drums like the ones shown here in a plaque from West Africa, formed a part of most public ceremonies or rituals.

Personal Appearance

Africa's warm climate meant that most people did not need many clothes. In the court of Benin clothes were not worn by men until they married. A Dutch writer noted that they only wore, '… a chain of corals or jasper round their necks.'

Special clothes and ornaments were reserved for the court. The public appearance of the King in Mali was described by a Arab scholar: 'On his head he has a golden skull-cap, bound with ends shaped like knives… His usual dress is a velvety red tunic.' In Benin there were guilds for weavers who wove and embroidered fine garments for the oba. Another guild of leather-workers made hats, fans and ornaments that were hung from the waist. The oba, in his full ceremonial costume, was an impressive sight: a crown of coral beadwork, a high collar of coral beads that reached from his shoulders to his chin, a necklace of leopard's teeth beneath the collar and coral necklaces hung over his chest. He wore ivory bracelets, an embroidered shirt and a skirt of woven textile.

▲ A king of Kush is shown on this slate tablet, dressed in a long robe. It is unlikely that ordinary people could afford such an item of clothing. The figure on the right is a lion-headed god called Apademak.

Closely cropped hair was the fashion in Kush, but sometimes a small knot was allowed to grow on top of the head. Royal Kush females liked to grow their fingernails long and henna was used to colour both nails and hair. Make-up on the face was also common. The Kush belief in life after death meant that personal items were buried with the dead. Jewellery was very popular and it is commonly found even in the graves of ordinary people. Bead necklaces of ostrich eggshells have been found, along with gold earrings and large metal bangles and anklets.

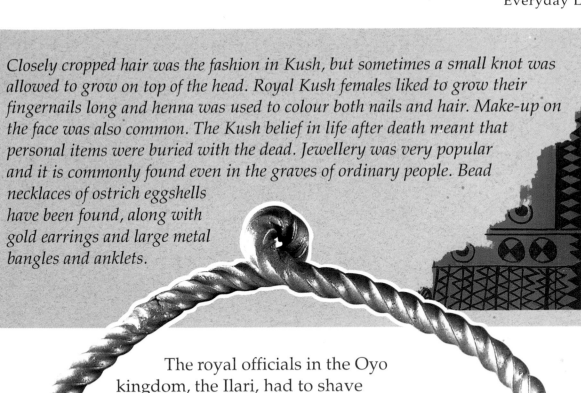

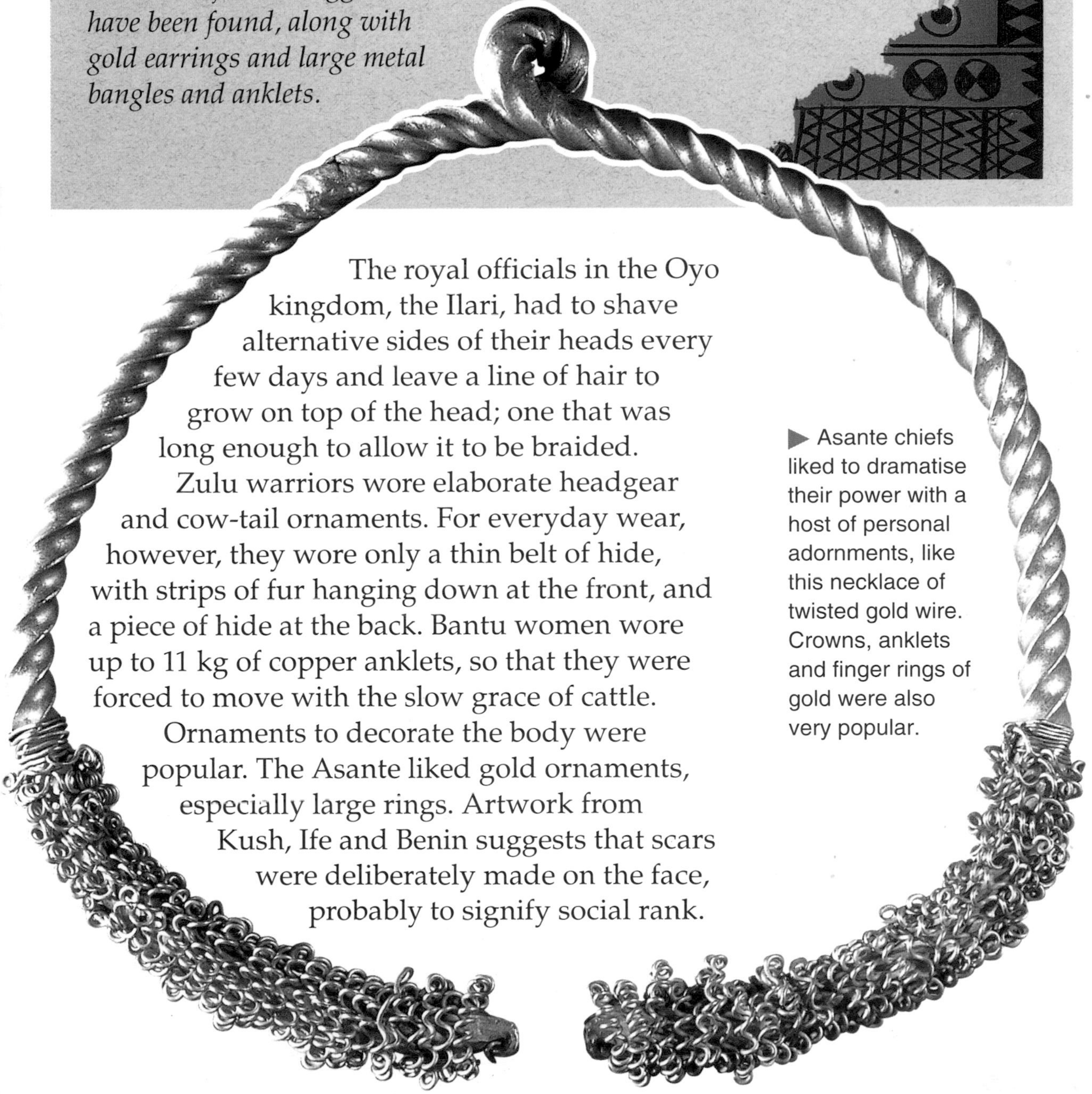

The royal officials in the Oyo kingdom, the Ilari, had to shave alternative sides of their heads every few days and leave a line of hair to grow on top of the head; one that was long enough to allow it to be braided.

Zulu warriors wore elaborate headgear and cow-tail ornaments. For everyday wear, however, they wore only a thin belt of hide, with strips of fur hanging down at the front, and a piece of hide at the back. Bantu women wore up to 11 kg of copper anklets, so that they were forced to move with the slow grace of cattle.

Ornaments to decorate the body were popular. The Asante liked gold ornaments, especially large rings. Artwork from Kush, Ife and Benin suggests that scars were deliberately made on the face, probably to signify social rank.

▶ Asante chiefs liked to dramatise their power with a host of personal adornments, like this necklace of twisted gold wire. Crowns, anklets and finger rings of gold were also very popular.

Slaves

As the various African kingdoms expanded and conquered new territory, they usually took prisoners. Some of these captives would be kept by the conquering kingdom and used to perform menial tasks like collecting firewood. Others were made slave soldiers in the army that had defeated them, but they could often look forward to eventually being freed. Around the end of the thirteenth century a freed slave even took control of Mali's army and governed the kingdom for a while. Mali also kept slaves on plantations, where they helped to produce food for the kingdom's towns.

When the trade routes across the Sahara desert became more important, under Muslim merchants, it became possible for states to export larger numbers of captives as slaves. Benin engaged in local trade, exchanging its captives as slaves in return for gold from the forest interior.

The arrival of Europeans on the west coast of Africa introduced a completely different kind of slavery. The owners of sugar, cotton and tobacco plantations in the Caribbean and the Americas wanted cheap labour, and Africa became the main supply source.

▼ Illustrations carved on this piece of ivory, from West Africa, show the plight of slaves, chained by the neck.

▶ The ill-treatment of slaves was one reason for the growth of the anti-slavery movement in the eighteenth century.

African kings and chiefs entered into a partnership with the Europeans, to supply slaves on a regular basis. They grew rich by organizing slave-hunting expeditions, and bringing the slaves to coastal towns, where they were branded and crammed into ships for the perilous journey across the Atlantic Ocean. Somewhere in the region of 10 to 12 million Africans landed in the Americas between the fifteenth century and the nineteenth. Many more were smuggled to the Americas. Another 10 to 12 million were said to have died on the journey. It is estimated that around 60 million Africans were forced to leave Africa.

While Benin was expanding and acquiring captives, it was happy to trade them as slaves with the Portuguese. When Benin's expansion ceased towards the end of the sixteenth century the source of slaves dried up and European traders looked elsewhere. As a result, rulers of kingdoms such as Oyo and Asante grew rich by supplying slaves.

A Frenchman described how the slaves were, 'marked on the breast with a red-hot iron, imprinting the mark of the French, English or Dutch companies, so that each buyer may distinguish his own.' An English captain of a ship described how the slaves were prevented from escaping from the ship: 'we shackle the men two and two while we lie in port and in sight of their own country, for 'tis then they attempt to make their escape, and mutiny: to prevent which we always keep sentinels upon the hatchways, and have a chestful of small arms, ready loaded...'

CHAPTER 9

The Legacy of the Kingdoms

Legacies of the African kingdoms are found all across modern Africa. Benin, now part of Nigeria, still has an oba and although he lacks the real power of a king, he has a political role in the state and still oversees civil disputes, religious rituals and ceremonies. When the British colony of the Gold Coast became the first African nation to achieve independence in 1957, it chose the name Ghana. Despite being hundreds of kilometres away from ancient Ghana, the new country drew symbolic strength by naming itself after West Africa's first mighty kingdom.

▼ The Oba of Benin (centre) with local chiefs, is still the focus of local ceremonies and rituals.

▲ The hustle and bustle of trade is as much part of Africa today as it was many centuries ago.

In southern Africa, Rhodesia, another former British colony marked its independence in 1980 by calling itself Zimbabwe – the name of its kingdom's royal court over a thousand years earlier.

The novelist Chinua Achebe (born in 1930) remembers how each year, before the harvest begun, a yam festival was held, 'to honour the earth goddess and the ancestral spirits of the clan. New yams could not be eaten until some had first been offered to these powers… All cooking pots, calabashes [dried gourds] and wooden bowls were thoroughly washed, especially the wooden mortar in which the yam was pounded… no matter how heavily the family ate or how many friends and relatives they invited from neighbouring villages, there was always a large quantity of food left over at the end of the day.'

Many of the traditional religious beliefs that we looked at earlier remain an important part of African thought. On the streets of modern Benin city, for example, one may find an altar dedicated to the god of blacksmiths, Ogun, filled with small piles of scrap metal. In modern Zimbabwe, spirit mediums are consulted to help communicate with ancestral spirits.

Many aspects of everyday life for Africans today are a reminder of the culture of past kingdoms. Men are still mostly the traditional farmers while women make the pottery that remains the essential equipment of households. Other areas of art, especially music and sculpture, continue to thrive in the heart of African culture and now reach out to other parts of the world. In the recent past, European artists like Picasso were hugely influenced by African sculpture. Today, people all over the world – and especially those of African descent – are discovering the heritage of the great kingdoms that once flourished across the continent.

▼ The rich and colourful culture of the African kingdoms lives on in the people of modern Africa.

Timeline

BC
3000 Egypt united as one kingdom.
800 BC–AD 250 Kingdom of Kush flourishes.
500 BC–AD 250 Nok culture in West Africa flourishes.

AD
700–800 Islam spreads into West Africa across the Sahara desert.
750 Kingdom of ancient Ghana at its height.
1200–1400 Kingdom of Great Zimbabwe at its height.
1350 Kingdom of Mali at its height.
1400 The Ife kingdom flourishing.
1440–1606 Rule of the warrior kings in Benin.

1464 Sonni Ali the Great becomes ruler of the Songhay kingdom.
1486 Portuguese traders make contact with Benin.
1640 Beginning of civil war in Benin.
1680 Asante states come together under the rule of one king.
1730 Oyo kingdom at the height of its power.
1818 Shaka becomes leader of the Zulu kingdom.

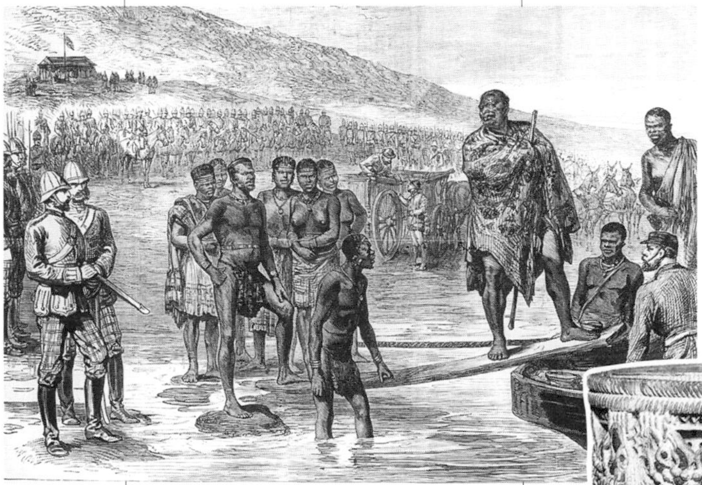

1874 Capital of Asante kingdom captured by the British.
1879 British army first defeated by Zulu army but then inflicts a crushing defeat on the Zulu kingdom that leads to its breakup.
1897 Benin captured and looted by the British.

1957 West African colony of the Gold Coast wins independence and names itself Ghana.
1980 Rhodesia becomes Zimbabwe.

Glossary

Alafin The title of the Oyo king.
Almoravids North African Muslim dynasty that conquered parts of ancient Ghana.
Archaeology The study of history by excavating and examining physical remains.
Asantehene Title of Asante kings between the end of the seventeenth century and the end of the nineteenth.

Bantu A large group of black people in central and southern Africa.
Bashorun The commander-in-chief of Oyo's armies.
Brass An alloy, or combination, of copper and zinc, used by artists in Ife and Benin to create sculptures.
Bronze An alloy of copper and tin.

Edo A West African people living in what was the Benin kingdom.

Ife The earliest kingdom to emerge in West Africa.
Ilari Officials who worked in the Oyo court.
Islam The religion of Muslims, as revealed by Mohammed the prophet of Allah.

Kumasi Capital city of the Asante kingdom.
Kumbi Saleh Capital city of ancient Ghana.

Manillas Horseshoe-shaped pieces of copper and brass used as a form of currency.
Mansa The title adopted by the kings of Mali.

Nok culture The name of a West African culture, from around 500 BC to AD 200, whose knowledge of iron-making techniques and terracotta art probably influenced later kingdoms.

Oba The title of the Benin king.
Oral tradition The keeping of historical records through generations of professional storytellers instead of through written accounts.
Oyo Mesi A council of important chiefs who advised the alafin of Oyo.

Shona Bantu people of southern Africa.
Soninke West African people who founded the kingdom of ancient Ghana.
Sudan A region of sub-Saharan Africa between the Atlantic Ocean and the Nile Valley, or a modern republic in north-east Africa that includes the land of the ancient Kush kingdom.

Terracotta A brownish-red form of clay that becomes hard after heating.
Tribute A regular payment made by one individual, or group of people, to another as a sign of dependence.

Warrior Kings Five obas who ruled Benin between the fifteenth and seventeenth centuries and expanded the kingdom's territory.

Yoruba An African people, once famous for their military skills, inhabiting the West African coast.

Zimbabwe A Shona word meaning 'royal court'.
Zulu A black South African people.

Further Reading

Eyewitness Guides – Africa by Yvonne Ayo (Dorling Kindersley, 1995)
African Designs by Rebecca Jewell (British Museum, 1994)
Ancient Ghana by Philip Koslow (Chelsea House Publishers, 1995)
Asante by Philip Koslow (Chelsea House Publishers, 1995)
Benin by Philip Koslow (Chelsea House Publishers, 1995)
Mali by Philip Koslow (Chelsea House Publishers, 1995)
Songhay by Philip Koslow (Chelsea House Publishers, 1995)
Yorubaland by Philip Koslow (Chelsea House Publishers, 1996)
Cultures of the World: Sudan by Patricia Levy (Marshall Cavendish, 1997)
Cultural Atlas for Young People by Jocelyn Murray (Facts on File, 1980)
Cultures of the World: Zimbabwe by Sean Sheehan (Marshall Cavendish, 1993)
Black Kingdoms, Black People by Anthony Atmore and Gillian Stacy (Orbis Publishing, 1979)
The Art of Benin by Paula Ben-Amos (Thames & Hudson, 1980)
An Outline History of Benin for Key Stage 2 by Andrew Forson, The Historical Association (Vale Packaging Ltd, 420 Vale Rd, Tonbridge, Kent TN9 ITD, UK)
African Arms and Armour by Christopher Spring (British Museum Press, 1993)
Benin: An African Kingdom (WWF UK Education Distribution, PO Box 963, Slough SL2 3RS, UK)
Benin Source Pack (A teachers' pack from The Northamptonshire Black History Group, c/o Wellingborough REC, Park Road, Wellingborough NN8 IHT, UK)
The Kingdom of Benin (A teachers' pack from Commonwealth Institute, Kensington High Street, London W8 6NQ, UK)

Index

Figures in bold are illustrations